Other books from the same Author.

1. **Dharma, The Categorial Imperative**; edited by Ashok Vohara, Arvind Sharma and Mrinal Miri; ISBN 81-246-0270-0
2. **A New Curve in the Ganges** — Mahatma Gandhi's Interpretation of Hinduism; by Arvind Sharma; ISBN 81-246-0271-9
3. **New Focus on Hindu Studies**; by Arvind Sharma; ISBN 81-246-0307-3
4. **World as Dream**; by Arvind Sharma; ISBN 81-246-0365-0
5. **The World as Image**; by Arvind Sharma; ISBN 81-246-0362-6

Sea-shell as Silver
A Metaphorical Excursion into Advaita Vedānta

Arvind Sharma
McGill University

D.K. Printworld (P) Ltd.
New Delhi

Cataloging in Publication Data — DK
[Courtesy: D.K. Agencies (P) Ltd. <docinfo@dkagencies.com>]

Sharma, Arvind, 1940-
Sea-shell as silver : a metaphorical excursion into Advaita Vedānta / Arvind Sharma.
vii, 110 p. 23 cm.
Includes bibliographical references (p.)
Includes index.
ISBN 8124603529

1. Advaita. 2. Vedanta. 3. Metaphor — Religious aspects — Hinduism. I. Title.

DDC 181.482 22

ISBN 81-246-0352-9
First published in India in 2006

Published and printed by:
D.K. Printworld (P) Ltd.
Regd. Office: 'Sri Kunj', F-52, Bali Nagar
New Delhi-110 015
Phones: (011) 2545-3975; 2546-6019; *Fax*: (011) 2546-5926
E-mail: dkprintworld@vsnl.net
Website: www.dkprintworld.com

Preface

Religious philosophies often resort to metaphors, allegories or examples to render their ideas credible. This seems to hold good not only for transtheistic systems of thought such as Advaita Vedānta but even for such theistic systems of thought as Christian theology. The doctrine of the trinity has enjoyed a special reputation within Christianity for abstruseness but its proponents helpfully point to the fact that if H_2O can exist in three states: as solid, liquid and gas in the form of ice, plain water and gas, without compromising its status as "water," — then surely three persons of the trinity need not compromise the oneness of God.

It is not only items within a tradition which we might find incomprehensible; sometimes even the tradition as a whole might invite this reaction. Thus people talk about the "scandal" of Christianity, namely, that God could become incarnate as a human being. Some have even urged that the claim may have to be believed simply because it is so extraordinary and that it is through faith that one accomplishes this. On the face of it, the Advaitin claim, that there is one undivided reality underlying this phenomenon of objects and other beings which we call the universe, is no less scandalous. The claim that all this diversity, which we see before our eyes and which is fundamental to our experience of the universe, is ultimately false is, in its own way, no less incredible than the Christian claim that God became man.

Advaita Vedānta tries to render these, and other propositions central to it, accessible by resorting to illustrations. One such example is provided by its use of the perceptual error, which makes us mistake a seashell for a piece of silver, as an illustration for enhancing the plausibility of several Advaitic ideas. This book is devoted to an exploration of the use of this illustration in Advaita Vedānta.

Contents

1

Introduction

I

One must begin by restating the basic premises of the system of thought known as Advaita Vedānta in order to fully understand the shell-silver metaphor in the context of that system. These premises are famously contained in the following verse:

ślokārdhena pravakṣyāmi
yadukataṁ granthakoṭibhiḥ
brahma satyam jaganmithyā
jivo brahmaiva nāparaḥ

T.M.P. Mahadevan paraphrases this verse as follows:

> Śaṅkara puts the entire philosophy of Advaita in half a verse where he says: *Brahman* is real: the world is an illusory appearance; the individual soul (*jīva*) is *Brahman* alone, not other. The non-duality of *Brahman*, the non-reality of the world, and the non-difference of the soul from *Brahman* — these constitute the teachings of Advaita.[1]

Students of Advaita will be quick to realize, however, that although this verse and the paraphrase summarize the basic tenets of the Advaita Vedānta succinctly, these tenets need to

1. T. M. P. Mahadevan, *Outlines of Hinduism,* Bombay: Chetana limited, 1971, p. 141.

be understood rigorously, and more rigorously than might be apparent at first sight.

This point applies particularly to the statement that the world is *mithyā* and the *jīva* is no other than *Brahman*. One must begin by recognizing what has been left unsaid in both the statements, for falsehood is often said to consist in the things not said. Thus when it is said that the world or *jagat* is *mithyā*, what has been left unsaid is that it is so in relation to *Brahman*, or to be more precise, that it is not *asat* but *mithyā* in relation to *Brahman*. The significance of this clarification becomes apparent when understood in the light of the following statement of M. Hiriyanna:

> Śaṅkara regards all diversity as being an illusion (*mithyā*). But it is very important to grasp correctly the significance of so describing it. Śaṅkara's conception of the real (*sat*) is that of eternal being, and *Brahman* is the sole reality of that type. Similarly, his conception of the unreal (*asat*) is that of absolute nothing. The world, in all its variety, is neither of the one type nor of the other. It is not real in this sense, for it is anything but eternal. Nor is it unreal in the sense defined, for it clearly appears to us as no non-entity can. Nobody, as it is stated in advaitic works, has ever seen or is ever going to see a hare's horn or barren woman's son. They are totally non-existent. Further it possesses, unlike non-entity, practical efficiency or has value, being serviceable in life. This is the reason why the world is described in Advaita as other than real and the unreal (*sadasadvilakṣaṇa*) or as illusory appearance. The serpent that appears where there was only a rope is neither existence nor non-existent. It is psychologically given (*prasiddha*), but cannot be logically established (*siddha*). In other words, the things of the world, though not ultimately real, are yet of a certain order of reality. They are appearances, in the sense that they depend for their being upon some higher reality. The "serpent", for

> example, points to the existence of the rope; and the dependence is one-sided, for while the disappearance of the rope necessarily means the disappearance of the serpent, the reverse does not hold good.[2]

The other statement: that the *jīva* is identical with *Brahman* also stands in need of clarification, as it is the *jīva* in its true essence, as *ātman*, which is identical with *Brahman* and not the *jīva* as is empirically encountered. The significance of this statement becomes fully apparent when it is understood in the light of the following explanation offered by M. Hiriyanna:

> This difference in the explanation has a vital bearing on the Advaita doctrine, and Śaṅkara consequently lays particular emphasis on it. It brings out clearly what is meant by identity of the *jīva* and *Brahman* which is of fundamental importance to the doctrine. The *jīva* is not false or illusory as the world is; for, if it were, there would be none to be saved and the whole teachings of the Upaniṣads would then be nullified. Salvation implies survival. The liberated *jīva* is not thus lost in *Brahman*. But, at the same time, it should be remembered that it would not be quite correct to say that it is preserved, for it is only as *Brahman* that it continues to be losing its limitations which are all false. The limitations, which are really of its empirical adjuncts, appear transferred to it as, in our second example of illusions, the yellowness of the glass appears transferred to the conch. We may thus take the ego as an appearance of *Brahman* in the second degree, and in not the first as the physical world is. The notion of the ego is accordingly that of a complex (*viśiṣṭa*), and points not only to an element which is identical with *Brahman* but also to limiting adjuncts like the internal organ.[3]

---

2. M. Hiriyanna, *The Essentials of Indian Philosophy*, London: George Allen & Unwin, 1949, pp. 155-56.
3. *Ibid.*, pp. 157-58.

The last line is the most significant for our purpose. It is not the *jīva* as *viśiṣṭa*, or as a complex which is identical with *Brahman*. As a complex it consists both of the part identical with *Brahman* as well as the internal organ. But the internal organ component of this complex is not identical with *Brahman*.

The distinction between this dual relationship of *Brahman* with the world and with the individual soul or *jīva* must be probed further to achieve a deeper understanding of the system for hermeneutical as well as philosophical reasons. Such an inquiry is important for hermeneutical reasons because of the sublime vagueness of the teachings of the Upaniṣads, which are more in the nature of inspired utterances than treatises of philosophy.

> This vagueness of the Upaniṣadic teaching is particularly in reference to the relation of *Brahman* to the individual soul on the one hand, and to the physical universe on the other. Though statements about their identity are more and prominent, those distinguishing them are not altogether wanting. The first problem to solve for anyone attempting to systematize the teachings of the Upaniṣads is accordingly to harmonize the two sets of statements.[4]

Śaṅkara's resolution on this point may be presented as follows:

> Śaṅkara recognizes. . . that there are two streams of thought in the Upaniṣads; but he thinks that one of them, viz. that which affirms the reality of diversity, is only a concession to empirical modes of thought. All diversity being thus only conditionally true, the only teaching of the Upaniṣads, according to him, is that of unity. Since, however, there can be no unity apart from variety, he does not describe his

4. *Ibid.*, p. 152.

> teaching as monism but only as "non-dualism" (*advaita*). Strictly speaking, it is therefore wrong to say, as it is now too common to do, that Śaṅkara teaches bare unity. If he did, his Absolute would be "pure nothing". But as Vācaspati says, he only denies the many but does not affirm the one.[5]

This statement, if not elaborated, leaves room for confusion because the manner in which Śaṅkara identifies the universe with *Brahman* is different from the manner in which he identifies the *jīva* with *Brahman*. Or to put it another way, the diversity referred to in the passage cited above encompasses two kinds of diversities — the diversity displayed by the various objects of the universe and the diversity displayed by the various individual subjects, who are also part and parcel of the universe. The manner in which the diversity of the objects of the universe is negated is somewhat different from the manner in which the diversity of the individual subjects is negated, although the two negations are not unrelated. Such a realization is crucial for a correct understanding of the scriptural exegesis of the Upaniṣadic texts carried out by Advaita.

The issue might appear as one of only dry intellectual interest, when presented in this way. It is, however, also loaded with deep philosophical significance, or is at least often viewed in that perspective.

We find ourselves existing in a universe full of material objects, although we ourselves live in it as conscious subjects. When our awareness of our environment and of ourselves rises to a point when we begin to ask searching philosophical questions about them both, then one form such an interrogation might assume is to raise the question: is there an ultimate

---

5. *Ibid.*, p. 154.

reality which underlies this material universe? We may also be led, similarly, to raise the question: is there an ultimate reality underlying all the conscious beings in the universe? These two lines of inquiry naturally suggest a third — the relationship of these two underlying realities, should they be successfully identified? The answer to these philosophical issues is at stake in the present discussion.

We move now back to the issue of the *Brahman* and the nature of its relation to the universe and the individual souls within it. It was emphasized earlier that the Advaitic conception of these two relationships is different. This difference needs now to be explained further. However:

> Before explaining this difference, it is necessary to draw attention to an important distinction between two types of illusions in common experience. A person may fancy that he sees a serpent at a distance, while closer scrutiny reveals to him that is only a rope. The later or correcting knowledge, like practically all knowledge of the kind, affirms the existence of something; but it contradicts the object *as that* (i.e., serpent) which appeared before. He says to himself or feels when he discovers his error: "It is a rope, not a serpent". Again a person looking at a white conch through a sheet of yellow glass, of whose existence he is not aware, takes it to be yellow. But a suitable change in his standpoint will disclose to him that the yellowness belongs to the glass and not to the conch. Here also, as in the previous case, the later knowledge affirms the existence of some reality; unlike it, however, it does not deny the object as which it appeared, viz. the conch, but only an *aspect* of it — its yellowness. He still sees it as a conch, but only adds that it is white and not yellow. The illusion in the first case consists of mistaking a given object for another that is not given; in the second, it consists merely in attributing to an object which is given, a feature that does not really belong to it, though it is also

> presented at the time. But for the interposition of a sheet of glass (*upādhi*) to which the yellow actually belongs, there would be no illusion at all in the later case.
>
> Now these types of illusion serves to illustrate the difference in the manner in which, according to Śaṅkara, one and the same *Brahman* comes to appear both as the world and as the individual self (*jīva*). It gives rise to the illusion of the world, as a rope does to that of the serpent in our first example.[6]

In the case of its relationship to the individual self, however, "the *jīva* is not false or illusory as the world."[7] "It is *Brahman* itself appearing through media or limiting adjuncts (*upādhi*)," but these "limitations which are really of its empirical adjuncts, appear transferred to it as in our second example of illusions, the yellowness of the glass appears transferred to the conch."[8] M. Hiriyanna clarifies the same point elsewhere as follows:

> **The World and the Individual**
>
> IT is well known that God, the individual soul and the world constitute the subject matter of all philosophy and religion. In monistic systems, however, where the only reality recognized is God or the Absolute, the remaining two terms of this trinity are necessarily to be reduced to it. The manner of doing it may be the same in the case of both of them, as it seems to have been in certain forms of Advaita that were once prevalent; but in Śaṅkara's doctrine, it is not so. Though the soul and the world are alike admitted in it to be not distinct from *Brahman*, which is the Upaniṣadic term for the Absolute, there is a difference in the way in which they are

6. *Ibid.*, pp. 156-57.
7. *Ibid.*, p. 157.
8 *Ibid.*, p. 158.

> explained to be so. The purpose of this short note is to indicate wherein this difference lies.
>
> We shall begin by drawing attention to two types of illusions in common experience. A person may fancy that he sees a serpent at a distance, while closer scrutiny reveals to him that it is only a rope. The later or correcting knowledge here, like practically all knowledge of the kind, affirms the existence of something; but it contradicts the object as that which appeared before. Again, a person looking at a white crystal through a sheet of yellow glass, of whose existence he is not aware, takes it to be yellow. But a change in his standpoint will disclose to him that the yellowness belongs to the glass and not to the crystal. Here also, as in the previous case, the later knowledge affirms the existence of some reality; unlike it, however, it does not deny the object as that which appeared, viz. the crystal, but only one aspect of it, the yellowness. The illusion in the one case consists in mistaking a given object for something else that is not given; in the other, it consists of merely in referring to an object, which is given a feature that does not really belong to it, though it also happens to be presented. But for the interposition of the object, to which the yellowness actually belongs and the percipient's ignorance, we should add, of the true color of the crystal, there would be no illusion at all in the later case. It is accordingly described as *sopādhika-bhrama* or an illusion involving the presence of an *upādhi*, which is the name given to such intervening factors. In the former, on the other hand, there is no such factor; and it is therefore described as *nirupādhika-bhrama.*[9]

Hiriyanna illustrates the first type of illusion with the example of the snake and the rope. The second type of illusion he

9. M. Hiriyanna, *Popular Essays in Indian Philosophy*, Mysore: Kavyalaya Publishers, 1952, pp. 49-50.

illustrates with the help of the example of a "white conch [seen] through a sheet of yellow glass."

This might seem like a modern example but it is really a restatement, in modern idiom, of a more traditional one. This fact is clearly acknowledged by Hiriyanna himself in another context, while explaining the doctrine of error as found in the Prābhākara school of Mīmāṁsā. He writes:

> One of the illustrations given in explaining this position, is a conch that is seen yellow by a jaundiced person. For the sake of simplicity, we shall make a slight alteration in it by supposing that the conch is seen through a yellow glass instead of by a jaundiced eye, and the fact of the existence of the glass is for some reason or other lost sight of.[10]

The point which might go unnoticed here is that while Hiriyanna developed his example of the white conch seen through a sheet of yellow glass in the context of his discussion on the theory of error in one school of Mīmāṁsā, he has used the same example as a substitute for another illustration of illusion used in Advaita Vedānta.[11]

We face somewhat of a problem here in making a traditional association of his specific illustration of the "white

10. M. Hiriyanna, *The Essentials of Indian Philosophy*, p. 156.

11. The question arises: which *traditional* example of *sopādhika bhrama* in Advaita has Hiriyanna in mind here? What Hiriyanna writes elsewhere may provide some clue here, as there are almost verbal similarities in the following passage to those passages cited earlier, almost to the point one might say that Hiriyanna is quoting himself:

> The *jīva* is not false as the world is, but only its limitations are so; and these limitations, which are really of its empirical adjuncts, appear transferred to it as, in our second example, the elements of the glass appears transferred to the crystal. It is for the purpose of elucidating this point that Śaṅkara, as explained by the →

conch seen through a sheet of yellow glass" but we are not without help. Hiriyanna is using it as a version of the second example cited by Śaṅkara (in his Introduction to the *Brahma-sūtrabhāṣya*) of the moon appearing (*candraḥ sadvitīyavat*) as double. Such a visual aberration would obviously be the result of an ocular defect and it was also an example of ocular defect that Hiriyanna had modified into one involving the "white conch scene through a sheet of yellow glass." The original example, it will be recalled, involved the case of one's vision being affected by jaundice.[12]

II

I would like to propose now that Hiriyanna could also have arrived at a similar result through a closer examination of the shell-silver metaphor.

Let me begin by freely admitting that the tradition in general does not encourage one to draw such a conclusion. In most of the traditional literature on the subject the rope-snake

---

→ commentators, gives two separate examples of illusion in the beginning of his commentary on the *Vedānta sūtra: śuktikā hi rajatavat avabhāsate, ekaś candraḥ sadvitīyavat iti* — "Mother-of-pearl appears as silver: and the single moon, as double." He refers to it elsewhere also in the same work, and we shall conclude by citing two of his statements relating to the concept of the *jīva*: "As long as it is associated with the adjuncts of *buddhi*, so long only is the *jīva* a *jīva*. In reality, however, there is nothing like *jīva*-hood apart from what is fancied to be such by reason of this adjunct." (II.iii.30). "The *jīva* is not other than the Lord, but yet its intrinsic omniscience and omnipotence are hidden from it because it falsely identifies itself with its bodily organism." (III. ii. 6). (M. Hiriyanna, *Popular Essays in Indian Philosophy*, p. 50).

12. M. Hiriyanna, *The Essentials of Indian Philosophy*, pp. 144, 156.

and shell-silver illustrations are both cited as alternative illustrations of the same type of illusion, cases in which *Brahman* appears as the world. It will be recalled that the salient feature of this type of illusion consists in taking an object as given when it is not given. When the rope is mistaken for snake, the snake as taken is given, while it is not given (the rope being the given here). Note that the illusion is total: the snake is seen all by itself, the rope is not seen at all. The shell-silver example has also been used to illustrate precisely this kind of phenomenon.[13]

I would now like to draw attention to the following fact: that among the two elements involved in the rope-snake illustration, namely the rope and the snake, and among the two elements involved in the shell-silver illustrations, namely the shell and silver, it might be possible to argue that the discontinuity involved in the apparent transformation of the rope into the snake is of a higher degree than the discontinuity involved in the apparent transformation of the shell into silver. Or, to put it differently, the element of congruity between the shell and silver is relatively greater than one might posit between the rope and the snake.

In the case of the rope-snake metaphor, for instance, the inert rope is transformed into a live snake. In the case of the shell-silver metaphor, however, and inert object, shell, is mistaken for another inert object, silver. If we analyze the phenomena represented by the two carefully, the objects in question may be said to possess (1) size, (2) shape, (3) colour, and (4) weight. The list is obviously illustrative rather than exhaustive, but it allows one to make the point that when what is first thought to be a piece of silver and is then found to be a piece of shell, its size and shape and colour remain

13. See M. Hiriyanna, *Outlines of Indian Philosophy*, London: George Allen & Unwin, 1932, pp. 353, 357.

more or less the same, but its weight turns out to be different, and it is this lightness which gives the illusion away.

The point can be made even more forcefully if one is allowed to tinker with the metaphor a little bit. Thus, the example works even better if we assume that the original shell was mistaken as a piece of silver cast as a shell. Let it then be so assumed. So now when a person "approaches the object, picks it up and discovers that is too light to be silver, he at once realizes that he was in error."[14]

What end, it might now be justly asked, is served by such an exercise and how is our understanding of Advaita Vedānta enhanced by the introduction of the new set of assumptions, however minor. In order to grasp its significance one needs to revert to the Advaitic view and to revisit it in general, with Hiriyanna when he writes:

> We now know the Advaitic world-view in general. *Brahman* is the sole reality, and it appears both as the objective universe and as the individual subject. The former is an illusory manifestation of *Brahman,* while the latter is *Brahman* itself appearing under the limitations which form part of that illusory universe.[15]

Thus the illusory universe now comes to possess a finer distinction. It stands forth as the illusory manifestation of *Brahman* but some parts of it *also* appear as limitations of the *jīva,* although continuing to remain part of the illusory universe in general as they do so.

This introduces a wrinkle in the situation which cannot be allowed to go unremarked, for it is precisely this point which

---

14. M. Hiriyanna, *Outlines of Indian Philosophy*, p. 352.
15. M. Hiriyanna, *The Essentials of Indian Philosophy*, p. 158, emphasis added.

requires that the relation of *Brahman* to the universe and *jīva* be understood differently. It is important enough to posses implications even for Advaitic epistemology. Hiriyanna writes:

> The cognitive situation is usually taken to involve a subject and an object. The Advaitin substitutes for them *dṛk* and *dṛśya*, the former meaning the self or what reveals, and the latter, what is revealed. The reason for the substitution is that the other division is not logically quite satisfactory. The subject includes not only *dṛk* but also *dṛśya*. It is really a complex of the self and the not-self. This is clear from the statements like "I know myself," where "myself" refers to some thought or feeling or, as Hume said, "some particular perception or other, of heat or cold, light or shade, love or hatred, pain or pleasure." These perceptions, being observable, are *dṛśya* and necessarily point to some center of consciousness beyond them.[16]

But to stay closer home, its significance comes to the fore in the concept of *itaretara adhyāsa* or the doctrine of mutual superimposition. Note that while the world may be a superimposition on *Brahman*, the statement cannot be reversed and *Brahman* cannot be considered a superimposition on the world in terms of Advaitic thought.[17] However, such a mutual superimposition between the *ātman* and the *anātman* is clearly spoken of in Advaita. In other words, the impossibility of such mutual superimposition in relation to the *Brahman* and

---

16. M. Hiriyanna, *Indian Philosophical Studies*, Mysore: Kavyalaya Publishers, 1957, p. 135.
17. This is not to say that the critics of Advaita cannot level this charge. Indeed Advaitic thought displays such a possibility. See M. Hiriyanna, *The Essentials of Indian Thought*, pp. 156, 162.

the world and its plausibility in relation to the *jīva* and the world are two facts which stand out in sharp contrast.[18]

This is where the significance of our modified version of the shell-silver metaphor becomes helpful. It can be used to explain the general picture both from the point of view of *Brahman* and the *jīva*. From the point of view of *Brahman* it functions in a way analogous to the rope-snake metaphor. But from the point of view of the *jīva* the rope-snake metaphor is of little help in understanding its world-view.

Even otherwise, the shell-silver metaphor may be helpful even in a way in which the rope-snake metaphor is not. For instance, it might enable one to accommodate the phenomenon of mutual superimposition which otherwise confounds rational accommodation. Mutual superimposition involves superimposing, for instance, the features of *antaḥkaraṇa* on the *ātman* and of the *ātman* on *antaḥkaraṇa*. Thereby the *antaḥkaraṇa* which is not spiritual in nature, appears conscious and the *ātman*, although infinite in nature, appears limited to the *antaḥkaraṇa*.[19] When the reality *Brahman* is "realized in one's own experience, what is denied is not *jīva* as a spiritual entity, but only certain aspects of it, such as its finitude and its separateness from other selves."[20] This corresponds to the case where the shape and form of shell and silver are recognized as *similar*, but the *difference* in weight is also recognized.

---

18. The contrast is more muted when one looks at both the world and the *jīva* from the standpoint of *Brahman*; it comes into clearer focus, if one looks at both the world and *Brahman* from the stand point of the *jīva*.
19. The rope-snake metaphor poses problems in this case.
20. M. Hiriyanna, *The Essentials of Indian Thought*, p. 157.

III

The difference between the two types of illusion may also be approached from another angle. This distinction, as noted earlier, is explained traditionally in terms of *nirupādhika* and *sopādhika bhrama.* Hiriyanna contrasts the difference between "taking as given what is not given at all" with "taking a feature of what is given as given, which is not given" in elaborating this point. There is also a third way, however, in which one might posit this difference — as involving a difference between total illusion and partial illusion.

Perhaps it is best to illustrate the distinction between the two with the help of an example. Let us suppose that, on a hazy day, on account of our vision being obscured by the haze, we momentarily mistake a lamp-post for a person. Then continuing on our journey on this foggy and rainy day we run into a person whom we momentarily mistake for a friend, until we realize that the person is not our friend but merely someone who looks like the friend. Upon returning home, somewhat crestfallen no doubt on account of these misadventures, we slip into a philosophical state of mind and start reflecting on these two misperceptions and the differences between them. We then realize that our first misperception — in which we mistook a lamp-post for a human being — could be characterized as total illusion, in a sense that there is little in common between the lamp post and a human being. Of course something has to be in common between two things, or at least in the circumstances surrounding them, for one to be mistaken for the other. We choose to overlook this aspect of the process common to all misperception (which possesses its own significance) to focus on the fact that we mistook two such dissimilar things as a living human being and an inert object for each other. It is the radical and total nature of this error which grasps our attention. By contrast, our mistaking the person on the road for a friend who looks like him or her involves a less radical error. Both of them are human beings and share many other attributes in common such as gender, height, disposition, gait etc. This is a case of partial error because we did not mistake what was not a human being for a human being, but rather one human being for another. In this sense it may be described as a partial illusion in comparison with what was called a total illusion earlier.[21]

The purpose of this new series of example is not merely to elaborate the distinction between the two types of errors but also to advance it. Let us now assume that we are on good terms with a family, which, somehow, for undetermined genetic reasons, consists of two sisters and two brothers, both of whom are identical twins. On account of the similarity to each others' features one could now easily occasionally mistake one of the brothers for the sisters. One could also, with even greater probability, mistake one brother for another or sister for another. We might wish to use the word *fractional* illusion to describe this situation, continuously with the cases of total and partial illusion spelled out earlier. One may wish to note, before one moves on, that the mistaking of one sister for

---

21. The fact that in the case of total illusion nothing of the original is left upon disillusionment and that in the case of partial illusion something of it is, should not be confused with the doctrine of causation as explained in Advaita Vedānta. The following extract may help avoid such confusion, which touches on the doctrines of *vivartavāda* and *pariṇāmavāda*:

    It is desirable to distinguish further between actual and apparent change. Actual change (*pariṇāma*) signifies that with a particular thing is destroyed, it does not disappear entirely. A rope when pulled to pieces remains as fibre. A pot, when broken, exists as potsherds. In apparent transformation (*vivarta*), on the other hand, the disappearance is complete. When the illusion of →

another or one brother for another is a more intimate kind of illusion than mistaking a brother for a sister or vice versa. When philosophical push comes to shove we may feel the need to distinguish between fractional and intimate illusion, with intimate illusion being regarded as a subset of fractional illusion.

These series of illusions could be characterized in yet another way — a fourth way. The first way of distinguishing between them was to describe them as *nirupādhika* and *sopādhika*; the second was to describe them as "taking as given what is not given" and "taking only a feature of what is given as given which is not given," the third was to describe them first as total and partial illusions, to which we also added the category of fractional illusions. A fourth way then would be to refer to this set of series of illusions in terms of a slightly altered vocabulary. In such a vocabulary the word *illusion* could be restricted in meaning to refer only to *total* illusion, while what we referred to as *partial* illusion would now denoted by the word delusion. Furthermore, in the same spirit, one could refer to what we have chosen to describe as fractional illusion, by the word *confusion*.

This new vocabulary might suggest that we are beginning to play word games. However, an exhibition of the possibility

---

→ "serpent" is overcome, there will be nothing of *it* left. It remains only to add that the *jīva* is not an effect in either of these senses. It is not a real transformation, nor even an illusory appearance of *Brahman*, so that no principle of causation is at all involved there. If we yet speak of the individual self as born, we only mean that its adjuncts like the physical body come into being and not the spiritual element in it. Hence the *jīva* is described as beginningless (*anādi*). It is, as already indicated, *Brahman* appearing in an empirical dress. (M. Hiriyanna, *The Essentials of Indian Philosophy*, pp. 159-60).

that the new vocabulary being employed might actually enhance our understanding of Advaita Vedānta should help dispel this impression. It should now be recalled that the *jīva* consists of two elements — *Brahman* as it is and the *upādhis* or adjuncts, which are part and parcel of the phenomenal universe. It is therefore described as *viśiṣṭa* or complex of the two.

The complex contains an element of confusion which takes the form of *con-fusion*. This point may now be elaborated further.

IV

Some schools of Hindu philosophy regard the ego "as a simple and ultimate entity. It is in fact synonymous with the self (*ātman*) in these doctrines. But the Advaitin denies the integrity of the self in this sense and takes it to be a complex of the *sākṣin* and the internal organ."[22] The two, according to it get identified with each other and the Advaitin

> ascribes the identification to an unconscious confusion between the entities involved, viz. body, senses, etc. on the one hand, and the *sākṣin* on the other. It accordingly involves, in his view, ignorance of the true character of these entities and is a case of error or *adhyāsa*. There are indeed occasions, he admits, when we do distinguish between two, as when we speak of "our body," but he explains them only as flashes of the truth which are soon veiled from us. This argument is applicable to the *antaḥ-karaṇa* also and when a person feels pain, for example, and says "I am suffering" he is illegitimately transferring to the true *ātman* what according to the previous reasoning belongs to *antaḥ-karaṇa*.[23]

22. M. Hiriyanna, *Outlines of Indian Philosophy*, London: George Allen & Unwin, 1932, p. 354.

23. *Ibid.*, pp. 355-56.

Thus there is con-fusion between the *sākṣī* and other aspects of our being, two of which are specified in the passage. These may broadly be referred to as body and mind.

What I would like to draw attention to is the fact that although both the body and the mind are in a sense "objects" for the *sākṣī*, there is a slight distinction in their nature as objects which bears examination. The body is an object in the objective sense, in the sense that I can see and feel it like an external material object. But the mind is an object in a very different sense. To the extent that I can think of myself I make myself an object of my thought and in this sense become an object for the *sākṣī*. But my body as an object and my mental images as an object are objects of two different kinds. I would now like to press the point further to claim that as a mental image I am closer to the *sākṣī* than as the body. I am indeed different from it as both body and mind, but if *sākṣī* is pure consciousness then mental consciousness, I submit, is closer to pure consciousness than physical consciousness, in the sense that it is less material in nature than the body (or even body-consciousness) and on account of this relativity greater immateriality closer to pure consciousness, which itself is totally immaterial, devoid as it is of both mental and physical objects.[24]

Another way of making the same point would be to say that the body is an object, which in the course of perception, is reduced to body-consciousness, while the mind is a kind of (reflected) consciousness which is objectified in the process of being perceived by the *sākṣī* as the ego.

---

24. *Ibid.*, pp. 355-56. Also see Andrew O. Fort, *The Self and Its States: A State of Consciousness Doctrine in Advaita Vedānta*, Delhi: Motilal Banarasidass, 1990, p. 5.

This is my reason for suggesting that while the rope-snake metaphor explains the relationship of the universe as such to *Brahman* adequately when it is stated that it "gives rise to the illusion of the world as the rope does the snake,"[25] the shell-silver metaphor probably captures the spirit of its relationship to the *upādhi*s more fully when it is stated that while the universe is an "illusory manifestation of *Brahman* (like in the snake of the rope), the [individual subject or *jīva*] is *Brahman* itself appearing under the limitations which form part of that illusory universe,"[26] as the relative closeness of silver to shell compared to that of the rope to the snake seems to throw more light on the relationship of *jīva* to "the limitations which form part of that illusory universe."[27]

To appreciate this point one may wish to view the shell-silver metaphor in two ways: once as capturing the relationship of *Brahman* to the universe, and once again as capturing the relationship between *Brahman* to the *jīva*'s "limitations which form part of that illusory universe."[28]

The first perspective, being the standard one, is more easily stated. Just as the illusion of silver obscures the nature of the shell, the universe obscures the true nature of *Brahman*. What is not given, namely silver, is taken as given. The subsequent knowledge, that it is shell, affirms the existence of something; but contradicts the object as such, namely, silver, just as the knowledge of the rope contradicts the object as such, namely, the snake.

It can also be argued, however, that this correcting knowledge, although it denies the object as such, recognizes certain correspondences between the two, such as in shape

---

25. M. Hiriyanna, *The Essentials of Indian Philosophy*, p. 157.
26. *Ibid.*, p. 158.
27. *Ibid.*, p. 158.

and form, so that some aspects of the object denied are not denied and it is these aspects which allow for the confusion between the *sākṣī* and the internal organ to occur resulting in *adhyāsa*.

Such a refinement of the point, however, must seem like gilding the lily unless its relevance to a proper understanding of Advaita Vedānta can be explained. One way in which such relevance could be established is the following.

The *jīva* has been described as *anādi* or beginningless in Advaita Vedānta, as more generally in Hindu thought. It seems to have gone unrecognized that the *jīva* can be understood as such in two senses in Advaita Vedānta. Hiriyanna explains one understanding of the statement as follows:

> These selves or *jīva*s differ from the common objects of experience in being coeval with time and not in it like them — a belief which the Advaitin shares with the followers of the other orthodox systems. Thus each of the indefinite number of selves we have assumed has been there from the beginning of time or is *anādi*.[29]

Elsewhere he explains the same point in more detail, in the more general context of the doctrine of karma as follows:

> Here, no doubt, a question will be asked as to when the responsibility for what one does was first incurred. But such a question is really inadmissible, for it takes for granted that there was a time when the self was without any disposition whatsoever. Such a view of the self is an abstraction as meaningless as that of mere disposition which characterizes no one. The self, as ordinarily known to us, always means a

28. *Ibid.*
29. M. Hiriyanna, *Outlines of Indian Philosophy*, p. 362; also see M. Hiriyanna, *The Essentials of Indian Philosophy*, pp. 159-60.

> self with a certain stock of dispositions; and this fact is indicated in the Indian expositions by describing karma as beginningless (*anādi*). It means that no matter how far back we traced the history of an individual, we shall never arrive at a stage when he was devoid of all character. Thus at all stages, it is self-determination; and the karma doctrine does in no sense imply the imposition of an actual constraint from outside. So deep is the conviction of some of the adequacy of karma to account for the vicissitudes of life and the diversity of human condition that they see no need, as we shall point out later, to acknowledge the existence of even God, conceived as the creator of the world and its controlling judge.[30]

It now needs to be recognized that the *jīva* is *anādi* in two other senses: it is beginningless in the sense that it is identical with *Brahman* in its true character and as *Brahman* is *anādi* or eternal, the *jīva* must be so. It is also beginningless however, in another sense, in the sense that in its false character as *jīva*, caught in *saṁsāra*, its involvement in this process is without a beginning as well. In keeping with these facts Śaṅkara accepts it as *anādi* in both the senses.[31] A more general consideration may also serve to strengthen the argument. The word *jīva* is really a contraction of the word *jīvātman* and while the form *jīva* possesses the merit of being more short and concise, the more cumbersome *jīvātman* conveys the fuller picture. In its capacity as *jīva*, the subjective individual is involved in *saṁsāra*; and in its capacity as *ātman* it is identical with *Brahman*. This double-barrelled approach fits in neatly with what has been and is about to be described.

---

30. *Ibid.*, pp. 47-48.

31. See M. Hiriyanna, *Outlines of Hinduism*, p. 362 note 3 and pp. 368-69.

Thus the *jīva* is *anādi* both as itself in a liberated state, and as *jīva* wandering around in *saṁsāra*. This dual relationship then turns out to be analogous to the notion of time as it applies to the universe and to *Brahman*. Note that in Advaitic metaphysics both the universe and *Brahman* are eternal. The difference between the two lies not in the fact but in the nature of their eternality. The universe is characterized by *pravāharūpa nityatā* or flowing eternality — like that of an unceasingly flowing river. *Brahman* is characterized by *kūṭastha nityatā* or transcendental eternality, more like that of an unvarying and unwearing rock. In terms of English usage the eternality of *Brahman* could be characterized as "permanent" and that of the universe as "constant."

If the dual character of the *anādi* nature of the *jīva* is thus recognized, and the dual nature of the eternalities involved in the case of the universe and *Brahman* as well, then perhaps the reader will be more receptive to the dual metaphorical use of the shell-snake metaphor as developed earlier.

V

The importance of the distinction between the two types of metaphors — the rope-snake and the tinted glass metaphor cited at the beginning of this chapter, also emerges in the context of the two ways in which the "great utterance" or *mahāvākya*: *tat tvam asi* (that thou art) has been interpreted. This is the famous statement repeated no less than nine times in the same context in the *Chāndogya Upaniṣad*.[32]

The point at issue is this: is this statement to be understood literally (*vācyārtha*) or metaphorically (*lakṣyārtha*)?

---

32. K. Satchidananda Murty, *Revelation and Reason in Advaita Vedānta*, Delhi: Motilal Banarasidass, 1974 p. 84.

One may begin by examining the position of Śaṅkara on this point. K. Satchidananda Murty notes:

> It is to be noted that Śaṅkara himself does not say that there is *lakṣaṇā* in his *Chāndogya Upaniṣad Bhāṣya* while expounding this text. In fact he expressly says that it is not a sentence to be interpreted as "you are a lion"; and he does not mention there the example of "This is that Devadatta" of which later Advaitins make so much. As in his opinion there is no word which can appropriately refer to *Ātman*, and as any word can only imply it and not signify it directly, there's no reason why any special difficulty should be felt about this single text. But Śaṅkara himself in his minor works says that "That Thou Art" is a *lakṣaṇā vākya* like "This is that Devadatta"; and as to why he said so has been explained away by Dharmarāja.[33]

The minor work referred to in the above passage is the *Vivekacūḍāmaṇi* (244-251).[34]

Two points immediately attract attention. The first has to do with the question of Śaṅkara's authorship of the *Vivekacūḍāmaṇi*. This is a disputed point in current scholarship[35] and the fact that Śaṅkara in his *Chāndogya Upaniṣad Bhāṣya* expressly argues against a *lakṣaṇā* interpretation,[36] while in the

---

33. K. Satcitananda Murty, *op. cit.*, p. 97.
34. *Ibid.*, p. 342 note number 16.
35. See Karl H. Potter, ed., *Advaita Vedānta up to Śaṅkara and His Pupils*, Delhi: Motilal Banarasidass, 1981, vol. I, p. 335.
36. K. Satcitananda Murty, *op. cit.*, p. 96. Also see p. 90:

    Śaṅkara says that this teaching of the identity of *Brahman* and the soul is not like the conception of Viṣṇu in an idol. The idol is looked upon and worshipped only as if it were Viṣṇu, for how can lifeless stone actually be Viṣṇu? He maintains that here we are not asked to think of the individual soul as if it is *Brahman*. It is categorically stated in the Upaniṣad that the real Self, the world-

→

Vivekacūḍāmaṇi he seems to endorse such an interpretation, weakens the case for his authorship of the latter.

The second, and in a sense more important point, is the attempt by Dharmarāja to challenge the *lakṣaṇā* interpretation. Dharmarāja came several centuries after Śaṅkara and during this interval the *lakṣaṇā* interpretation gained much ground. The effort by Dharmarāja to favor the literal interpretation may indicate the reassertion of this tradition going back to Śaṅkara.

Dharmarāja bases his argument on the linguistic claim "that words directly referred to the substantives and not to the attributes of the substantives, and that when words have to

→ ground (*jagato mūlam*) itself, *is* the individual soul. Nor is this statement to be understood in a metaphorical way, like the saying, "You are a lion," because the text emphatically says that as clay is the one thing to be found in all products of clay, the one thing "Being" alone is real. Further, it is said that liberation is delayed only so long as there is no true knowledge of this, for as soon as there is such knowledge, bondage comes to an end. Hence the knowledge that each of us is *Brahman* cannot be merely metaphorical. It cannot be also taken as mere praise, for it is no compliment for the All-Self (*sarvātmaka*) *Brahman* to be praised as Śvetaketu; nor is anyone interested in praising Śvetaketu, to whom "That Thou art" is addressed. To teach this cardinal truth — the identity of the soul and *Brahman* — is the aim of all the Upaniṣads. So when the Upaniṣads affirm "That Thou art!," the idea "I am the Real Being" cannot but arise in one's mind and since the Upaniṣads are a *pramāṇa*, this idea can never afterwards be destroyed. A critic may ask: if every man is the Real Being, why does he not *know* himself to be so? Śaṅkara replies that this is not a real difficulty, because usually a man does not have even the idea that he is an agent or an enjoyer, apart from the consciousness of his material body and senses. Since he has the idea that his body is himself, it is no wonder if he does not realize himself as the Real Being. The sentence "That Thou art" removes this false idea.

refer to attributes, they do so by implication."[37] The identity in the statement: *That Thou Art*, is an assertion of identity between bare substantives, and "there is no contradiction in syntactically connecting two substances to posit their identity when they are *also* signified by the express sense of the words."[38] Thus

> According to Dharmarāja, the right example for *jahadajahallakṣaṇā* is a sentence of the sort, "See that crows do not eat this curd". Here the word "crow" abandons its usual expression and takes on an implied meaning, for it refers to all animals and birds, which are likely to snatch the curd, e.g., parrots, cats, dogs, etc. The purport of the sentence is that the curd should be kept safely without allowing any animals and birds to touch it, and not that crows alone should not be allowed to touch it. Thus, as Dharmarāja says, here the word "crow" implies "spoiler of curd" (*dadhyupaghātaka*), crow as well as not-crow. In "That Thou art" and "This is that Devadatta," Dharmarāja does not find any such implication, and so they are not proper examples of *lakṣaṇā vākya.* He says that the statement of earlier teachers (*sāmpradāyikāḥ ācāryāḥ*) that "That Thou art" is a *lakṣaṇā vākya* is only a tentative admission in the course of argument (*abhyupagamavāda)*, and not the final conclusion.[39]

K. Satchidanda Murty also notes that:

> A recent commentator of the *Vedānta Paribhāṣā* has explained why "That Thou art" should not be taken as a *lakṣaṇā vākya.* According to him, in "The hamlet is on the Ganges," we take "Ganges" to imply the bank of the Ganges, because we

37. *Ibid.*, p. 96.
38. *Ibid.*
39. *Ibid.*, p. 97.

> already know that there cannot be hamlets on rivers, but only on their banks. Since we do not know the identity of *Brahman* and jīva before hearing "That Thou art," why should we reject the express sense? On the contrary, if one already knows this identity, he is in fact *mukta* (liberated soul), and for him the sentence is useless. So this commentator argues that through its express sense itself the sentence is able to convey us the great truth.[40]

It is a matter of some interest then that given these facts the *lakṣaṇā* explanation of the *mahāvākya: tat tvam asi,* should have emerged.

And it emerged early. Sureśvara, usually regarded as a direct disciple of Śaṅkara, establishes the meaning of the *mahāvākya* by invoking *lakṣaṇā*. He does so by distinguishing between two ways of understanding the meaning of a sentence, "through the well-known meanings of the words constituting it"[41] and "through the meaning which are related to the well-known meanings of the words constituting it."[42] The first is referred to as *muhkya vṛtti* and the second way is referred to as *lakṣaṇā vṛtti*. The next step consists of distinguishing among different kinds of *lakṣaṇās*.

Lakṣaṇā is said to be of four kinds: (a) *jahallakṣaṇā,* (b) *ajahallakṣaṇā,* (c) *jahadajahallakṣaṇā,* (d) *gauṇa vṛtti.* In (a) the usual well known (*prasiddha*) meaning is put aside and a meaning related to it is taken, e.g., in "There's a hamlet on the Ganges," the word "Ganges" does not signify its usual or referent, the river Ganges, but a bank on it. In (b) the usual meaning as well as the meaning related to it are taken, e.g., "The lances are coming," the word "lances" without forgoing

40. *Ibid.*

41. *Ibid.*, p. 91.

42. *Ibid.*

its usual meaning signifies the "lance-bearers." In (c) a part of the usual meaning is left out, and a part of it is retained, e.g., in "This is that Devadatta," differences in the accidental qualities of Devadatta are ignored, and Devadatta himself is taken as the referent. In (d), the meaning intended is apprehended and through its relation to the quality of a thing, e.g., in "Devadatta is a lion," the intended meaning, grasped through the quality of "courage" is found in both of them.[43]

Two questions now arise in the context of the *mahāvākya* under discussion: why should *lakṣaṇā vr̥tti* apply to it and not *muhkya vr̥tti,* and should it be the case that *lakṣaṇā vr̥tti* must be applied, which kind of *lakṣaṇā* needs to be applied.

In relation to the first question it is pointed out that in common parlance the word that refers to the cause of the world is *Saguṇa Brahman* (and not *Nirguṇa Brahman*). Similarly the word *thou* refers to a person's body (or body-mind complex) and not to the *ātman*. Note that common usages of the two terms are being applied here. As this is not the Advaitic position, which identifies (*nirguṇa*) *Brahman* with *jīva* as *ātman,* the other route which employs an implied sense must be taken.

As to which of the four forms of *lakṣaṇā* applies in this case, it is example (c) — that of Devadatta — which is utilized by the proponents of this view. The point is explained as follows:

> Suppose two persons have seen one Devadatta at some place and time and that later the same two people have come across the same Devadatta at another place and time. Of the two, one may recognize him to be Devadatta, while the other may not. Then the first would tell the second, "This is that Devadatta." Here the former does not mean that the two places and times are the same, nor does he mean that the

43. *Ibid.*

> two Devadattas under those two conditions are not in the same respects different. Devadatta when previously seen may have been very stout and wearing a striped shirt, while Devadatta later might be lean and wearing a white shirt. The statement does not mean that the stout Devadatta wearing a striped shirt is in all respects the same as the lean Devadatta wearing the white shirt; but what is recognized as the same is the person Devadatta, who is accidentally characterized by stoutness or leanness, with white shirt or striped shirt. So when it is said "This is that Devadatta," no identity is posited between the leanness of Devadatta and the stoutness of Devadatta. Omitting these accidental qualities (leanness, stoutness, etc.), what is qualified by them is asserted to be the same.[44]

The point to note here is that, as Devadatta's example illustrates, the assertion is not tautologically vacuous.

> The Advaita school says that there is no tautology in this sentence; otherwise "recognition" (*pratyabhijñā*) would also involve tautology. As in recognition, from the statement also no new knowledge is obtained; but it removes the mistaken notion of difference. One may know the nature of *Brahman* and also the nature of the individual self, and yet one may think the two to be different, just as we may have seen a man previously and see him again now and yet failed to cognize his identity. But when we are reminded of our having met that person previously, then we shed the mistaken idea that the person whom we met then and the person whom we meet now are two different persons; and in the same way, the Upaniṣadic sentence removes the delusion of difference between *Brahman* and the individual soul, even though their identity is known as soon as the true nature of both is known.

---

44. *Ibid.*, p 92.

> For, *Brahman* is the self of all, and the Self is not really the body or the ego, but Being.[45]

Hence the conclusion is drawn that the *mahāvākya* is to be understood as an example of *jahadajahallakṣaṇā*. As Satchidananda Murty explains:

> So, Sureśvara concludes, since "That Thou Art" gives us knowledge, unattainable from other sources, which directly leads to liberation, and as it is a declaration of the infallible Veda, the words "That" and "Thou," without abandoning their own sense, through their implied sense (*jahadajahallakṣaṇā*) sublate all contrary ideas. In his opinion, this sentence is like this sentence, "The *snake* is a rope" addressed to a man, who mistakes a rope for a snake; and the word *snake* in the sentence does not have for its referent a real snake, as is usually the case, but that thing in front – a rope. Similarly, according to Sureśvara, "Thou" does not signify the thing, which is usually called the self, but the Self as it is really.[46]

The point of interest for us here is that Sureśvara has used the rope-snake metaphor as the route through which to assert the identity of the *jīva* with *Brahman*. But the identity of the *jīva* with *Brahman* is that of taking a feature of something given as not given, as illustrated by the yellow-tinted conch analogy and not that of taking as given something which is not given at all. Hiriyanna says that "We may take the ego as an appearance of *Brahman* into second-degree, and not in the first as the physical world is."[47] But because Sureśvara has chosen to work at the level of, and with an example of, the "first-degree," he had to use the path of *lakṣaṇā vṛtti*. He's not wrong

45. *Ibid.*, pp. 92-93.

46. *Ibid.*, p. 94.

47. M. Hiriyanna, *The Essentials of Indian Philosophy*, p. 158.

in doing so as the limiting adjuncts (*upādhis*) also form part of the illusory universe, but in choosing to view them vertically and not laterally as mutually superimposed with *ātman*, he has had to take the longer route. The rope and snake cannot be viewed as in a state of mutual superimposition, for the snake is superimposed on the rope but not vice-versa. In the case of *anātman* and *ātman* components of the complex of the *jīva*, however, such mutual superimposition is possible.

The interesting point is that if one turns to the text itself, the nine examples clarify the nature of *nirguṇa Brahman* rather than that of the *jīva*.[48] This lack of parallel clarification of the *jīva* may be one reason why Sureśvara chose to adopt the course he did.

However, as the context is one of ultimate teaching and as the question of the ultimate nature of the human being has *already* been similarly identified in the preceding passages,[49] it stands to reason to take the identity as directly expressed. The context is two-fold: the search for the ultimate ground of the individual subject and the search for the ultimate ground of the objective universe. And the two (*tvam* and *tat*) are identified. Although this conclusion has been reached, and reinforced, on the basis of the two examples distinguished by Hiriyanna as correctly representative of the relation in Advaita Vedānta between *Brahman* and the objective universe on the one hand, and between *Brahman* and the subjective individual on the other, namely, the rope-snake example as illustrative of the former and the yellow-tinted conch of the latter, yet Hiriyanna himself interprets this seminal utterance of *tat tvam asi* not so much as representing the identity of *nirguṇa Brahman*

48. S. Radhakrishnan, ed., *The Principal Upaniṣads*, Atlantic Heights, NJ: Humanities Press, 1996, pp. 458-76.

49. *Ibid.*, pp. 450-58.

and the pure *ātman*, as between *Īśvara* or God and *jīva*. It is perhaps useful to document this fact on account of its ability to surprise. Thus at one point Hiriyanna writes:

> Just as the whole universe is the effect of *māyā*, the proportions of the universe which constitute the gross and subtle bodies of an individual self are conceived as the effects of that particular self, *avidyā*. In fact, the relation of *Īśvara* to the world is exactly parallel to that of the jīva to its organism. Considered apart from these individual and cosmic accompaniments, the *jīva* and *Īśvara* are one or, more strictly, are not different. That is the significance of *tat tvam asi*. The *jīva*s which we have assumed to be many are in consequence only empirically so; and the individuality characterizing each is due to its adjuncts such as the body and the senses. Intrinsically they are but one, for each is alike the supreme Reality.[50]

Similarly, he also declares elsewhere

> Just as the whole universe is the effect of *māyā*, the portions of the universe which constitute the accompaniments of an individual self, like the physical body and the internal organ, are regarded as derived from the *avidyā* of that particular self. Whatever distinction there appears to be between the ego and the qualified *Brahman* or between one ego and another, is entirely due to these differing adjuncts. In themselves, the egos are not distinct from one another or from the qualified *Brahman*. The identity of the denotation of the two terms, *jīva* and the qualified *Brahman*, while their connotations are different, is the advaitic interpretation of "That thou art" (*tat tvam asi*). It does not mean, as it is so often represented to do, that man and the qualified *Brahman* or God (to use a term which we will soon explain) as such

---

50. M. Hiriyanna, *Outlines of Indian Philosophy*, p. 364.

> are one. Such an attitude is blasphemous, according to Advaita, as it is according to any religion or purely theistic doctrine.[51]

It cannot be denied that the option to interpret the identity in this manner is possible, given the structure of Advaitic thought available to us. But is it called for in this context, when it is possible to read in the *mahāvākya* the statement directly, that "the individual self when seen *sub specie aeternitatis*, is *Brahman* itself."[52]

VI

The next point, however, has to be developed not in the context of the identification of the self and *Brahman* but in the context of their empirical differentiation.

In the empirical sense, the subject and the object confront each other as the individual subject and the objective universe. From the point of view of Advaita Vedānta, however, the individual subject needs to be differentiated further. It is this fact which has led Advaitins to refer to the subject as *dṛk* rather than *pramātā*.[53]

---

51. M. Hiriyanna, *The Essentials of Indian Philosophy*, pp. 163-64.
52. *Ibid.*, p. 157.
53. M. Hiryanna, *Indian Philosophical Studies*, Mysore: Kavyalaya Publishers, 1957, p. 134. As M. Hiriyanna states elsewhere, "whatever we think of is for that very reason objective (*dṛśya*) and it cannot therefore be an element in that which is never presented as an object (*dṛk*)" (M. Hiriyanna, *Outlines of Indian Philosophy*, p. 373). One may now place the statement alongside that "things arising from *māyā* are all known (*dṛśya*) and to that extent at any rate they cannot be unreal, for the absolutely unreal, like "the hare's horn is only words." Nor can they be as real in their own right, for they are objective (*jaḍa*) and hence depend entirely on the spirit for their being" (*Ibid.*, p. 364)

Just as a subject has to be differentiated between that part of it which sees but cannot see itself (*ātman*), and that part of it which is seen within (*anātman*), the objective universe also needs to be differentiated between the purely objective universe and that part of it which has become the empirical adjunct of the *jīva* as the *upādhis*. Just as one distinguishes between *pramātā* and *dr̥k*, with *dr̥k* constituting a narrower slice of *pramātā*, a part of the *jagat* gets sliced off to become the subjectively objective universe of my mind, my feelings, my thoughts.

A correlation is now established between the subject and the object in Advaita Vedānta, which differs somewhat from the way in which the two are normally pictured and which provides for an overlap of subject and object on the margin of each. It is thus worth noting that "from it [*māyā*] spring into being not only organic bodies that house *jīvas* but also all inorganic nature."[54]

This distinction between organic and inorganic nature is significant, for what is inorganic can only be involved in one-way superimposition, not mutual superimposition. There can be no direct mutual superimposition between the purely organic and the inorganic. Thus one first superimposes the internal organ on the self and then, by "an opposite process" one superimposes the self on the internal organ. As Śaṅkara writes in his introduction to his commentary on the *Brahma-Sūtra*:

> . . . And we said that superimposition means the cognition of something as some other thing. Thus in accordance as one's wife, children, or other relatives are hale and hearty with all their limbs intact or as they suffer from the loss of

---

54. M. Hiriyanna, *Outlines of Indian Philosophy*, p. 364.

> those limbs, one thinks, "I myself am hale and hearty" or "I myself am injured"; thus one superimposes external characteristics on the self. Similarly one superimposes the characteristics of the body when one has such ideas as "I am thin," "I am fair," "I stay," "I go," or "I scale." So also one superimposes the attributes of the senses and organs when one thinks, "I am dumb," "I have lost one eye," "I am a eunuch," "I am deaf," or "I am blind." Similarly one superimposes the attributes of the internal organ such as desire, will, doubt, perseverence, etc. In the same way, one first superimposes the internal organ, possessed of the idea of ego, on the self, the witness of all the manifestations of that organ; then by an opposite process, one superimposes on the internal organ, etc. that self which is opposed to the non-Self and which is the witness to everything. Thus occurs this superimposition that has neither beginning nor end but flows on eternally, that appears as the manifested universe and its apprehension, that conjures up agentship and enjoyership, and that is perceived by all persons.[55]

The issue is not one of priority but of the difference in the nature of the elements involved. What Swami Gambhirananda says elsewhere provides a good example here.

> For instance, "I am this body," where the body as such is superimposed on the self, conceived of as "I." Or "This body is I," where a relationship with the self is superimposed on the body.
>
> For instance, "This is my body," where the attributes of the body are superimposed on the self. In the first case the separateness of the body and self is forgotten; in the latter they are kept apart, but the attributes get mixed up.[56]

---

55. Swami Gambhirananda, tr., *Brahma-Sūtra-Bhāṣya of Śrī Śaṅkarācārya,* Calcutta: Advaita Ashrama, 1977, pp. 5-6.
56. *Ibid.*, p. 1 notes 4 and 5.

Be it noted that although Śaṅkara only talks specifically of mutual superimposition in the case of the internal organs (*antaḥkaraṇa*), it also applies to the body and to the senses, For instance, "I am this body," where the body as such is superimposed on the self, conceived as "I." Or, "This body is I," where a relationship with the self is superimposed on the body.[57]

VII

We are now in a position to unveil the main point of this part of the disquisition: that in the light of what has been said hitherto, the Introduction to the *Brahma-Sūtrabhāṣya* of Śaṅkara can now be seen in a new light.

To begin with, it is worth noting that although Śaṅkara is writing an Introduction to a treatise on *Brahman* — the text itself being known as *Brahma-Sūtra* — he starts out by talking about *ātman* rather than *Brahman* in the Introduction. It is true that the two are identical but the fact that the ultimate ground can be approached from either end is of significance here. This need not come entirely as a surprise as the text is also optionally known as *Śārīraka-Mīmāṁsā* or the investigation of the "embodied *ātman*." The question to ask is — given both these possibilities, why did Śaṅkara choose the latter approach as the starting point when the text itself starts with *Brahman*?

But of even greater importance is the fact that in the Introduction itself Śaṅkara speaks of *avidyā* rather than *māyā*; and focuses, especially towards the end, on *itaretara adhyāsa* rather than just *adhyāsa*. The point is that he is heavily involved

57. *Ibid.*, p. 1 note 4.

in discussing the *jīva* as distinguished from *jagat*, or just the universe.

It is in this context that *his* use of the two examples of the illusion in the Introduction gains significance. Hiriyanna explains the significance as follows:

> It brings out clearly what is meant by the identity of the *jīva* and Brahman which is of fundamental importance to the doctrine. The *jīva* is not false as the world is, but only its limitations are so; and these limitations, which are really of its empirical adjuncts, appear transferred to it as, in our second example, the yellowness of the glass appears transferred to the crystal. It is for the purpose of elucidating this point that Śaṅkara, as explained by the commentators, gives two separate examples of illusion in the beginning of his commentary on the *Vedānta-sūtra: śuktikā hi rajatavat avabhāsate, ekas candraḥ sadvitiyavat iti. . .* "Mother-of-pearl appears as silver; and the single moon, as double." He refers to it elsewhere also in the same work, and we shall conclude by citing two of his statements relating to the conception of the *jīva*: "As long as it is associated with the adjunct of *buddhi*, so long only is the *jīva* a *jīva*. In reality, however, there is nothing like *jīva*-hood apart from what it is fancied to be such by reason of this adjunct." (II. iii. 30). "The *jīva* is not other than the Lord, but yet its intrinsic omniscience and omnipotence are hidden from it because it falsely identifies itself with its bodily organism." (III. ii. 6).[58]

---

58. M. Hiriyanna, *Popular Essays in Indian Philosophy*, p. 50. This passage was also cited earlier in part. Also see Anantanand Rambachan, *Accomplishing the Accomplished: The Vedas as a Source of Valid Knowledge in Śaṅkara*, Honolulu: University of Hawaii Press, 1991, p. 109.

The point to be noted here is that Śaṅkara gives the example of the two moons usually to illustrate the nature of existence of the *jīvanmukta*, of someone who is about to enter or has entered the state of realization and yet continues to witness[59] the apparent diversity of the universe, as in his gloss on *Brahma-Sūtra* IV. 1. 15.

Although one would not wish to be dogmatic on this point, it is clear that in Śaṅkara's writings certain illustrations are distinguished by certain connotations. Thus the illustration of the rope and the snake seems to orientated towards describing the status of the world in relation to *Brahman*, that of the shell and the silver that of the *jīva*, and that of the double moon that of the *jivanmukta*. Seen in this light it now becomes clearer why Śaṅkara should cite these two stock examples in his introduction to the *Brahma-Sūtra Bhāṣya*.

The development of the idea of mutual superimposition is important. Śaṅkara takes the appearance of the universe on the underlying *Brahman* as comparable to the appearance of the snake on the rope. But although he takes up the question of the superimposition of universe on *Brahman*, he does not take any account of the possible superimposition of *Brahman* on the universe. On the other hand, he discusses the cases of both the superimposition of the *anātman* elements on the *ātman* (symmetrically with that of the universe on *Brahman*) but then, in this case, he *also* discusses the opposite, the superimposition of the *anātman* on the *ātman*!

Initially this might appear as far out as the case of the superimposition of *Brahman* on the universe but Śaṅkara takes up the challenge here:

59. See Andrew O. Fort, *Jīvanmukti in Transformation: Embodied Liberation in Advaita and Neo-Vedānta*, Albany, N.Y.: State University of New York Press, 1998, p. 232 note 31.

> *Opponent*: How, again, can there be any superimposition of any object or its attributes on the (inmost) self that is opposed to the non-Self and is never an object (of the senses and mind)? For everybody superimposes something else on what is perceived by him in front; and you assert that the self is opposed to the non-Self and is not referrable (objectively) by the concept "you."
>
> The answer (of the *Vedāntin*) is: The self is not absolutely beyond apprehension, because it is apprehended as the content of the concept "I"; and because the self, opposed to the non-Self, is well known in the world as an immediately perceived (i.e., self-revealing) entity. Nor is there any rule that something has to be superimposed on something else that is directly perceived through the senses; for boys superimpose the ideas of surface (i.e., concavity) and dirt on space (i.e., sky) that is not an object of sense perception. Hence there is nothing impossible in superimposing the non-Self on the self that is opposed to it.[60]

It is striking that the examples of a snake being mistaken for a rope, or silver for a shell, are not discussed here. For instance, consider the following two examples.

> According to *Anyathākhyāti*, subscribed to by the Nyāya-Vaiśeṣika schools, we have at first a vague awareness of "this" with regard to the rope in front. As the mind is not satisfied with this alone, it craves for a distinct perception. But some defect in the cognizer, his instruments of perception, or environment debars this, at the same time that the similarity of the rope and the snake calls up the memory of the latter. This memory conjures up the visual perception of the snake, and so the "this" is apprehended as "This is a snake." According to some Buddhists who

60. Swami Gambhirananda, ed., *op. cit.*, p. 3.

> hold the *Anyathākhyāti* theory of error, the "this" of the externally perceivable rope is superimposed on the mentally present snake to form the erroneous judgment, "This is a snake." Their psychological explanation is this: It may so happen that owing to the past impression inherent in consciousness, there may be a simultaneous flow of the consciousness of the external "this" and the internal snake, in which case the two get mixed up. The Buddhists call this *Ātmakhyāti*.[61]

The point of the second example could as well have been illustrated by saying that the snake was mistaken for a rope by using the same psychological explanation.

In the case of neither of the two traditional illustrations — rope-snake or shell-silver — is the superimposition reversed, but I would like to argue that Śaṅkara's use of the shell-silver in his introduction to the *Brahma-Sūtra* is suggestive of the superimposition of the *anātman* on *ātman* (which are capable of mutual superimposition) as distinguished from that of the universe and *ātman* (= *Brahman*) (which are not). I base this claim on the use the verb *bhās* in the statement: *śuktikā hi rajatvat avabhāsate.* One can read here a hint of the insentient *anātman* element shining forth with consciousness superimposed upon *it*. The same statement would be harder to make of *jaḍa jagat*, which only "appears" on the underlying *Brahman*.

The point thus is based on two considerations: one hypothetical and the other hermeneutical. The hypothetical argument is that mutual superimposition is more easily imagined in the case of shell-silver than rope-snake. The hermeneutical argument is that the property of *bhāsa* or shine associated with silver has more in common with consciousness and thus the conscious agent called *jīva* than the inert *jagat.*

---

61. *Ibid.*, p. 2 note 8.

2

The Shell-Silver Metaphor and the Adhyāsa-bhāṣya of Śaṅkara

THE use of the shell-silver metaphor in the context of *adhyāsa* in Advaita has already been alluded to. The use of the metaphor in the context of *adhyāsa*, however, deserves to be investigated more thoroughly, if for no other reason than the fact that Śaṅkara specifically cites this analogy in his discussion of *adhyāsa* in the introduction to the *Brahma-sūtrabhāṣya*.

Śaṅkara's Introduction

> It is a matter not requiring any proof that the object, and the subject whose respective spheres are the notion of "Thou" (the Non-Ego) and the "Ego," and which are opposed to each other as much as darkness and light are, cannot be identified. All the less can their respective attributes be identified. Hence, it follows that it is wrong to superimpose upon the subject — whose Self is intelligence, and which has for its sphere the notion of the Ego — the object whose sphere is the notion of the Non-Ego, and the attributes of the object, and vice-versa to superimpose the subject and the attributes of the subject on the object. In spite of this it is on the part of man a natural procedure — which has its cause in wrong knowledge — not to distinguish the two entities (object and subject) and their respective attributes, although they are absolutely distinct, but to superimpose upon each the characteristic nature and the attributes of the other, and

> thus, coupling the Real and the Unreal, to make use of expressions such as "That am I," "That is mine." — But what have we to understand by the term "superimposition?" — The apparent presentation, in the form of remembrance, to consciousness of something previously observed, in some other thing.[1]

Although the actual reference to the shell-silver metaphor is made by Śaṅkara later in the Introduction, even at this point his position can be restated conveniently in terms of that metaphor, but it must be clearly recognized before this is attempted that "the opening passage in the *adhyāsa-bhāṣya*," cited above, "where it is stated that the Self and the not-Self are opposed to each other like light and darkness, is part of the objection; it is not *siddhānta*."[2] This is often overlooked. The issue here is the superimposition of the Self (*ātman*) and the not-Self (*anātman*). "A preliminary objection may be raised: how can there be reciprocal superimposition of the Self and the not-Self which are opposed to each other like light and darkness? The reply is: they are not opposites. Rope and snake, or nacre and silver are not opposites; the former in each case serves as the substrate on which the latter appears. What are opposed to each other are the final mode of the mind which has taken on the form of the Self (*akhaṇḍākāra-vṛtti*) and the other modes of the mind which take the phenomenon to be real (*viśaya-vṛtti*s)."[3] The point is perhaps best illustrated in terms of the shell-silver metaphor. Both shell and silver are

---

1. Eliot Deutsch and J.A.B. van Buitenen, *A Source Book of Advaita Vedānta*, Honolulu: The University Press of Hawaii, 1971, p. 152.
2. T.M.P. Mahadevan, *Superimposition in Advaita Vedānta*, New Delhi: Sterling Publishers Private Ltd., 1985, p. 17, note 3.
3. *Ibid.*, p. 4.

not opposed as objects of two different kinds; they are both solid objects and one, the shell, serves as the substrate of the other — silver.

Nevertheless it is by no means obvious, nor is it accepted by all, that the description of the opposition of the Self and the not-Self in terms of light and darkness is to be taken only as a preliminary view meant to be set aside later. T.M.P. Mahadevan is aware of this and remarks on the significance of taking this photic dualism literally: "What is considered by the objector to be the most serious charge that can be levelled against the concept of superimposition is this: that Self and the not-Self are opposed to each other like light and darkness. Since they are of contradictory nature there can be no identity between them i.e., the one cannot be superimposed on the other therefore the metaphysical superimposition of the Self and the not-Self is impossible."[4] His response is two-fold. The first response is to deny the stark nature of the opposition as discussed above, but he then proceeds to offer a second response which tries to accommodate the literal opposition implied in the contrast of light and darkness. Thus he writes: "We have already observed that according to Advaita, the Self and the not-Self are not opposed to each other like light and darkness and that the not-Self is only an appearance of the Self. Admitting, for the sake of argument, that the Self and the not-Self are of contradictory nature we reply as follows."[5] The reply offered then runs as follows:

> Superimposition, in the case of the Self, is certainly in conflict with reason. It does not brook inquiry. It is because of this superimposition that it is stated to be indeterminable (*anirvacanīya*). Logic has its limitations. It cannot cancel the

4. *Ibid.*, p. 16.
5. *Ibid.*

> perceptually experienced fact of superimposition. Reason, however, can testify to the fact of nescience, although it cannot account therefor. The postulation of *avidyā* or nescience is by its very nature inscrutable. To the intellect it seems to be a welter of contradiction. Advaita is aware of the inherent disabilities of the intellect. In the subsequent chapters we shall use reason, as far as it can go, in explicating the concept of superimposition or nescience, and when we come to a point where it has to stop, we shall try to indicate why it has to stop, and then consider how superimposition can be got rid of and the eternal Self realised.[6]

One must wonder if it is time to jump ship yet, because there is one vital difference between the Self and the not-Self and light and darkness. Light and darkness cannot coexist simultaneously, for darkness must disappear at the very approach of light. But the Self and not-Self are found to coexist simultaneously, indeed in a state of mutual superimposition which is not possible in the case of light and darkness. However, although light and darkness cannot coexist, light and shadow can. Indeed the shadow depends for its existence on light and finally merges into it when the sun is at the zenith. Thus, in this sense, while light and shadow may be a better metaphor for the relationship of the Self and the not-Self in some ways over that of light and darkness, nevertheless, inasmuch as the shell-silver metaphor approximates the empirical reality of the relationship of the Self and the not-Self, it seems to possess an advantage over that of light and darkness as both shell and silver can simultaneously be given in experience.[7] Or, to put it another way, mutual

---

6. *Ibid.*, pp. 16-17.
7. M. Hiriyanna, *Outlines of Indian Philosophy*, p. 351 ff.

superimposition does not occur "between the real and the real (light/darkness) or between the unreal and the unreal (two images reflecting each other) but between the real and the unreal. It is the task of metaphysics to identify the real."

What is at issue here is the nature of the relationship between the real and the unreal. What Śaṅkara implies by the opposition between light and darkness, I think, has to be understood in a "subjective sense." It is true that while in "ordinary usage we regard mental states as subjective, and physical states as objective. . . from the metaphysical point of view both orders of phenomena, material and mental, are equally objective."[8] It seems to me, however, that by using the word subjective here in the ordinary sense an important insight may be gained. If we examine the phenomenon of superimposition closely from an Advaitic perspective in the context of the subjective as ordinarily understood, we can distinguish between five superimpositions: (1) *transferring the qualities of outer things to the Self*, as "when it goes ill or well with his "son or wife and the like"; to say 'it goes ill or well with me'";[9] (2) *transferring the qualities of the body to the Self*, as when one says "I am fat, I am thin, I am white, I stand, I go, I leap"; (3) *transferring the qualities of sense-organs to the Self*, as when one says "I am dumb, impotent, deaf, one-eyed, blind"; (4) *transferring the qualities of the inner organ to the Self*, as when one desires wishes, doubts, resolves; and (5) *transferring the "subject" presenting the "I" (ahaṁ-pratyayaviṣaya) to the inner soul (ātman).*

All these five are *anātman* as distinguished from the *ātman*. If now by *viṣayī* in Śaṅkara's gloss one understands the *ātman*

8. S. Radhakrishnan, *Indian Philosophy*, London: George Allen & Unwin, 1962, vol. II, p. 612.

9. Paul Deussen, *The System of the Vedanta*, tr. By Charles Johnson, Chicago: Open Court, 1943, p. 54, note 29.

then it can be plausibly maintained that Śaṅkara here "declares that the subject and the object are opposed like light and darkness, so that what is truly subject can never become an object."[10] The following comment by Hiriyanna is also helpful here, wherein he offers two explanations of the distinction between the Self and the not-Self, one based on syllogistic and the other on analogical reasoning.

> The first step in understanding the Advaitic truth, as we have just stated, is to discriminate well between the Self and the not-Self, which are commonly confounded with each other; and the process is called *śodhana* or "clarification of the concept of the Self." To state, in the traditional form, one line of the argument used in this connection: "The body is not the Self for it is knowable, like (say) a jar." The general principle on which this argument is based, as indicated by the reason assigned, viz., knowability, is that the knower and the known are distinct or, more strictly, not identical — a principle which goes back to a much wider one that all transitive action involves elements which are not the same. The reasoning here may appear to involve no analogy, and therefore to be of the first type; but it is not so, for the contrast drawn in it is not between the knower and the known or the subject and the object, as required by the principle in question; it is between the components of the former, viz. the transcendental or ground self and the body, of which it is not the knower but merely the witness. Here the transcendental self, unlike the subject, is not accessible to common experience; and we are therefore transferring a principle which holds good in the empirical sphere to one beyond it. Hence the reasoning is of the second type.[11]

---

10. S. Radhakrishnan, *op. cit.*, vol. II, p. 477.
11. M. Hiriyanna, *Indian Philosophical Studies*, p. 47.

I suggest that perhaps the point could be settled in this manner — that there is the contrast between that of light and darkness when the distinction is understood in the second sense; but not in the first. And moreover, that the whole tenor of the passage, quoted below in another translation, is more in keeping with the first rather than the second interpretation and therefore the oppositional metaphor of light and darkness is the absolute[12] and not the preliminary view. This is at least one way in which what Hiriyanna calls the "shorthand style"[13] of Śaṅkara in the "preamble to the commentary on the Vedānta Sūtra"[14] may be deciphered. But the movement away from this absolutist position is almost immediate as a perusal of the whole passage will indicate. For if Śaṅkara stuck to the polarity between the *ātman* and *anātman* and did not introduce the intermediate category of *mithyā* — that is, if he insisted on the opposition of light and darkness and did not allow for the twilight zone, *saṁsāra* and *mithyā jñāna* would be hard to explain.

> Object (viṣaya) and Subject (viṣāyin), he says at the beginning of his work, having as their province the presentation of the "Thou" [the no I] and the "I," are of a nature as opposed as darkness and light. If it is certain that the being of the one is incompatible with the being of the other, it follows so much the more that the qualities of the one also do not exist in the other. Hence it follows that the transfer (*adhyāsa*) of the object, which has as its province the idea of the "Thou," and its qualities to the object, is logically false. Yet in mankind this procedure resting on false knowledge (*mithyā jñāna-nimitta*) of pairing together the true

12. The Ātman alone is truly real, at the subjective level, and from its point of view nothing else is, as darkness does not exist for light.
13. M. Hiriyanna, *The Essentials of Indian Philosophy*, p. 161.
14. *Ibid.*

> and untrue [that is, subjective and objective] is unborn (*naisargika*), so that they transfer the being and qualities of the one to the other, not separating object and subject, although they are absolutely different (*atyanata-vivikta*) and so saying, for example: "This am I," "That is mine."[15]

The introduction of the shell-silver metaphor in the next paragraph opens up the *anātman* for explication. At the "subjective" level in the traditional sense a binary opposition could work, but when the whole realm of mental and material is treated as equally objective then the category of *mithyā*, and its classic illustration of shell-silver, come into play. As Hiriyanna explains:

> The next step in understanding advaitic truth is to repudiate as false the not-self, which has thus been discriminated from the self; and the argument used for it runs as follows: The whole of the objective world is an appearance for it is the not-self, like shell-silver. Here the analogy is drawn not from the sphere of normal experience as in the previous case, but from that of perceptual illusion. The falsity of the silver that may be seen where there is only shell is verifiable at the level of everyday experience; and there is consequently no difficulty in accepting it. But no such verification is conceivable as regards the falsity of the things constituting the not-seif, so long as we continue to think under ordinary human conditions. Yet, if we extend to it on the basis of analogy the principle observed in the sphere of illusion, we may come to see that all that is objective, whether it is an adjunct of the self like the physical body or is a part of the external world like a jar, is an appearance. Such an argument may not give us certitude; but it can show that there is nothing necessarily absurd in the advaitic conclusion.[16]

---

15. Paul Deussen, *op. cit.*, pp. 53-54.
16. M. Hiriyanna, *Indian Philosophical Studies*, p. 48.

This text and the context in which it is lodged permit one to elaborate the exposition in terms of the shell-silver metaphor. Take, for example, the definition of *adhyāsa* as "apparent presentation, in the form of remembrance, to consciousness of something previously observed in some other thing." The element in the definition one wishes to focus on is the fact that superimposition has a nature like that of recollection.

> In the example of nacre-silver the silver that is cognised is illusory. It is superimposed on nacre that is real. Thus, in superimposition, there is the coupling of the true and the untrue, the real and the unreal. The real silver that was seen before, remains in the form of memory. The observer of nacre-sliver does not see that experienced real-silver. Nor does he recognise it as a mere recollection. Were it so, he would not actually see silver in the place where nacre is. The silver that he now sees, therefore, is not real and is indeterminable. The locus of superimposition here is nacre; what is superimposed is silver. The superimposition is not recollection; it has a nature which is like that of recollection.[17]

We now go to the next section of Śaṅkara's Introduction.

> Some indeed define the term "superimposition" as the superimposition of the attributes of one thing on another thing. Others, again, define superimposition as the error founded on the non-apprehension of the difference of that which is superimposed from that on which it is superimposed. Others, again, define it as the fictitious assumption of attributes contrary to the nature of that thing on which something else is superimposed. But all these definitions agree in so far as they represent superimposition as the apparent presentation of the attributes of one thing in another thing. And therewith agrees also the popular view

17. T.M.P. Mahadevan, *Superimposition in Advaita Vedānta*, pp. 1-2.

> which is exemplified by expressions such as the following: "Mother-of-pearl appears like silver," "The moon although one only appears as if she were double." But how is it possible that on the interior Self which itself is not an object there should be superimposed objects and their attributes? For every one superimposes an object only on such other objects as are placed before him (i.e. in contact with his sense-organs), and you have said before that the interior Self is well known to exist on the notion of the Ego, and the interior Self is well known to exist on account of its immediate (intuitive) presentation. Nor is it an exceptionless rule that objects can be superimposed only on such other objects as are before us, i.e. in contact with our sense-organs; for non-discerning men superimpose on the ether, which is not the object of sensuous perception, dark-blue colour.
>
> Hence it follows that the assumption of the Non-Self being superimposed on the interior Self is not unreasonable.[18]

As we are particularly concerned with the use of the shell-silver metaphor at the moment a few preliminary observations may be made with a view to clarify the nature of the problem with which we are concerned here. When a person cognizes a rope as a snake or a piece of shell as silver, he commits perceptual error. So the first point to be noted is that we are concerned here only with perceptual error. Secondly, erroneous cognition has an objective reference. It points to an object, e.g., a snake or silver, which a person claims to see, though the object in front is only a rope or shell. Thirdly, the object is directly cognized as something which exists then and there. The cognition of the object is thus characterised by immediacy. Fourthly, the cognition of the object is followed by a correction through the sublating cognition (*bādhaka-jñāna*).

---

18. Eliot Deutsch and J.A.B. van Buitenen, *op. cit.*, p. 152.

Though the object is seen at first as silver, subsequently it is seen in its true nature as shell. The cognition of shell which arises subsequently sublated the earlier cognition of silver; and so it is called the sublating cognition (*bādhaka-jñāna*). The explanation of the problem of error thus must take into account the points mentioned above.[19]

Then Śaṅkara goes on to refer to some other descriptions of superimposition. These have been identified with some well-known theories of error or *khyātis*[20] in Indian thought. Although he seems to offer three statements, according to Swami Gambhirananda "four alternative theories follow successively. Of these the first two. . . are comprised within the first statement." These four theories are those of *anyathākhyāti, ātmakhyāti, akhyāti* and *asatkhyāti*. All of these can be explained with the help of the shell-silver metaphor. According to *anyathākhyāti*.

> an illusion is the manifestation of a real object in the form of a different object. It is the misapprehension of one thing as another thing. The illusion consists in identifying two different things. It is presentative or perceptual in character. We wrongly perceive silver in nacre. This wrong perception of the silver in nacre is a case of illusion. It arises in the form "this is silver" (*idam rajatam*). Now the question is: how such an illusion arises? The Nyāya school points out that we first perceive an object which is white. This whiteness or brightness is common to both nacre and silver. We do not perceive the distinctive quality of the nacre owing to some defect in the eye. Owing to this defect, we miss the distinctive feature.

---

19. R. Balasubramanian, *Advaita Vedānta*, Madras: University of Madras, 1976, p. 38.
20. T.M.P. Mahadevan, *Superimposition in Advaita Vedānta*, p. 3.

> As a result the present brightness leads us to the recollection of the bright silver seen in the past. The idea of silver is revived in memory by association. Thus the perception of silver in a nacre depends on the extraordinary contact (*alaukika-sannikarṣa*) between the sense-organs and the object. Here is no ordinary contact (*laukika-sannikarṣa*) between the sense-organ and the object. The real silver and silverness come to be connected with the sense-organ through an extraordinary contact called *jñāna lakṣaṇa*. It is by means of this extraordinary contact, that the idea of silver reproduced in memory by association causes the visual perception of silver in nacre. Thus, the Naiyāyikas hold that the misapprehension of nacre as silver is due to the extra-ordinary sense-object contact.[21]

Attempts have been made to explain the doctrine of *ātmakhyāti* also with the help of the shell-silver metaphor. This theory is associated with the Yogācāra school of Buddhism. "According to the Yogācāra school, the silver is in the form of subjective idea which wrongly appears to be an objective fact. This objectification of the subjective idea is due to the sub-conscious impression (*vāsanā*) of silver. This sub-conscious

---

21. B.N. Singh, *Indian Logic*, Varanasi: Asha Prakashan, 1986, p. 27. The question could be asked: what is the object of illusion (*ālambana*)? "Jayanta discusses the alternatives of object. First, it may be said that silver, which occupies another space and time, accounts for the perception of silver at this spot and at this time. This alternative is untenable as it is the perception of a non-existent object like the sky lotus. Secondly, it may be said that nacre conceals its distinct form and assumes the form of silver. This is also untenable as we have no ground to know that the presentation of silver really refers to nacre. Thirdly, it may be said that the stimulating object is one and it appears in a different form. It is the wrong apprehension or misapprehension of the real form of the object" (*Ibid.*, pp. 27-28).

impression is beginningless (*anādi*) and is the result of nescience (*avidyā*). It is due to this idea of silver in our mind. This mental idea of silver appears wrongly as an object silver. Thus the objective appearance of a subjective idea is illusion."[22]

It is interesting, however, that no mention has been made of the shell in the entire exposition. Some critics see a problem here. If the Yogācāra school holds that all cognitions cognise only their own forms and not objects, then the cognition itself is a cogniser and the cognised one. If cognition cognises its own forms, there would be no distinction between illusory and valid cognition. Illusion as a form of invalid cognition cognises its own form as the valid cognition. How can we distinguish between the two?[23]

It seems the explanation along the following lines would do more justice to the Yogācāra position: "It may so happen that owing to past impression inherent in consciousness, there may be a simultaneous flow of the consciousness of the external "this" (shell) and the internal silver and the two get mixed up."[24]

According to the *akhyāti* theory associated with the Prābhākara school of Mīmāṁsā:

> in the nacre-silver illusion, the nacre by virtue of its lustre which it has in common with silver, is mistaken as silver on account of obscuration of memory. Further, Prabhākara holds that the sublating cognition does not contradict illusion, but recognises the distinction between the presentative and representative elements. When the distinction between the two is recognised, we have the

---

22. M. Hiriyanna, *The Essentials of Indian Philosophy*, London: George Allen & Unwin, 1949, p. 30.

23. *Ibid.*, p. 31.

24. See Swami Gambhirananda, tr., *op. cit.*, p. 2 note 8.

> sublating cognition "this is not silver." This happens only when one wants to pick up the silver, but fails. He finds only a piece of nacre. He then realises that "this is not silver."[25]

The fourth theory referred to was *asatkhyāti*. "This is associated with the Mādhyamika school of Buddhism according to which the non-existing silver appears as the non-existing nacre."[26] In the interest of comprehensiveness, the presentation of these theories of error in terms of the shell-silver metaphor may be rounded off by presenting the Advaitic doctrine of *anirvacanīyakhyāti* in the same metaphorical garb.

> The Advaita school holds that the object of illusion is neither real (*sat*) nor unreal (*asat*) nor both real and unreal (*sadasat*). It is different from both existence and non-existence (*sadasadvilakṣaṇa*). It is not existent or real because it is sublated or contradicted. The error is immediately rectified when we get true knowledge of the object, i.e., when we truly know that it is shell and not silver. Thus the knowledge of silver vanishes when the knowledge of shell arrives. This

---

25. B.N. Singh, *op. cit.*, p. 32. The theory of *akhyāti* has been criticized in terms of the shell-silver metaphor by Maṇḍana who "brings out the untenability of the Prābhākara theory of *akhyāti* yet in another way. A person who wants to drink water takes a tumbler and finds inside it a white, bright piece (shell). It is the idea of water that is in his mind. Since silver is not recollected by him at the time, non-discrimination between the two, i.e. silver and shell, is ruled out, and hence the shell inside the tumbler should not be mistaken for silver. However, such a mistake takes place. If any error should arise at all in the present case, it should be the erroneous cognition of water, for it is water which is remembered, and the person fails to notice the difference between the remembered and the perceived." (R. Balasubramaniam, *op. cit.*, p. 48).
26. Swami Gambhirananda, tr., *op. cit.*, p. 3 note 10.

> sublating experience shows that the object of illusion is not existent or real. Had it been real or existent, it should not have been sublated and contradicted. Secondly, it is also not unreal or non-existent because it appears in experience. And what is totally non-existent, like a barren woman's son, can never appear in experience to any one. The immediately perceived presence of the illusory object can never be said to be both real and unreal because it is a contradiction in terms to speak of a thing as both real and unreal. Therefore, the silver in illusion is really indeterminable as real or unreal. It means that the object of illusion cannot be logically defined as real or unreal.[27]

There are, however, problems in pushing the model of perceptual illusion in this context, for they place the locus of error in the object, not in the percipient, whereas the essential metaphysical error of conflating the *ātman* and *anātman* has its locus in the percipient.

These limitations of the shell-silver analogy in relation to *adhyāsa* are such as Śaṅkara seems to be aware of himself, as he also provides the examples of moon appearing as double or the sky appearing like a dome. That is precisely because certain objections could be raised to the shell-silver analogy in the context of the Self and the not-Self.

One of them is: In all cases of superimposition two objects are involved, one of which is superimposed on the other. In the case of the Self-not-Self, we do not have two realities. According to Advaita, the Self is the only reality. How, then, can there be superimposition when there is no entity other than the Self? As if in reply to such an objection, Śaṅkara gives the empirical example of the single moon appearing as if double. Here, there are no two objects involved, one being

27. B.N. Singh, *op. cit.*, p. 35.

superimposed on the other. The single moon appears as if double.[28]

There is also room for a much more serious objection. In all cases of superimposition there should be an object perceived. In the instance of rope-snake, the rope-substance is perceived as "this," its general nature; only its special character which is "rope-ness" is not perceived. This is not so in regard to the metaphysical superimposition of Self-not-Self. The Self is not an object of perception, it is not seen in front of us. The reply may be given in two stages: (1) Ether is not an object of perception, being supersensible. Yet unthinking people superimpose thereon curved surface, impurities, etc. and say it looks like a dome; one sees in it dust, clouds, etc. (2) The Self is above subject and object, the empirical Self becomes the object of the concept "I" because of being endowed with egoism, etc., which constitutes "not-Self." Moreover, also the inner Self is immediately realised.[29]

The fact that the inner Self is immediately realized ties back into the argument that the light-darkness metaphor overstates the contrast between the Self and the not-Self. Mahadevan states at one point:

> Here it may be noted that there can be no object seen without the seer and that even in the absence of all objects the seer sees. The Self is called "seer" only so long as it is the witness of objects or their absence (as for instance in deep sleep). But when there is nothing to be seen or witnessed even the terms "seer" and "witness" lose their meaning. The terms "seer" refers to the Self meaningfully as long as there is the seen. The distinction that is made between the two is not from the

28. T.M.P. Mahadevan, *Superimposition in Advaita Vedānta*, p. 4.
29. M. Hiriyanna, *The Essentials of Indian Philosophy*, London: George Allen & Unwin, 1949, p. 163, 166.

> final standpoint. *As we observed in the first chapter regarding the opening words of Adhyāsa-bhāṣya, to say that the Self and the not-Self are opposed to each other like light and darkness is not the siddhānta but the prima facie view, because there is no not-Self apart from the Self.* Even so we would here like to make it clear that the seen is not apart from the seer as it is only an appearance. That is why the term sight, meaning pure consciousness, is a better term for the Self than even the expression seer.[30]

The shell-silver metaphor may be used to further probe the nature of superimposition. The conditions required to be present for superimposition are said to be the following according to Advaita Vedānta: "(1) In order to superimpose an illusory object on a substrate, there must be the residual impression of having perceived that object earlier as real. (2) Defect in the object of cognition. (3) Defect in the cogniser. (4) Defect of the instrument of cognitions. (5) A knowledge of the general nature alone of the substrate without the knowledge of its particulars."[31] All of these can be illustrated with the help of the shell-silver metaphor in the following manner.

> (1) Silver is superimposed on nacre only by him who has seen real silver earlier, and not by him who has never seen silver. In order that silver may be superimposed on nacre one must also possess the residual impression caused by the prior knowledge of real silver. (2) There should be some defect in the object of cognition, e.g., similarity between what is superimposed and the substrate. A serpent is not superimposed on nacre nor is silver imposed on a rope, because there is no similarity between the two in each case. (3) There must also be in the subject who superimposes such defects as greed. (4) Besides,

30. T.M.P. Mahadevan, *Superimposition in Advaita Vedānta*, p. 24, emphasis added.

31. *Ibid.*, p. 13.

> there should be defects in the instruments of cognition such as eye-disease, insufficient light, etc. (5) And finally the substrate must be cognised in its general nature and its particularities must remain obscured. What is seen in front must be cognised as "this" and not as "nacre." If nacre be not apprehended as "this" there would be no superimposition. Nor could there be superimposition if what is in front be cognised as nacre.[32]

Mahadevan tries to show that each of these can be challenged in the case of the Self and refutes the challenges. (1) If nothing other than the Self is real, how does the superimposing Self have the residual impression of a real object? The condition, however, says that the object has to be perceived as real, it does not have to be real. It is "not necessary that one should have seen silver earlier in order to superimpose silver now on nacre. The silver that he saw earlier might also have been an illusory object . . . indeed, in the case of the illusory cognition of nacre-silver, what is superimposed is the identity of the real and the non-real, the nacre and the silver."[33] (2) How can one predicate defect of the Self? "In non-dual Self there is the defect which is called nescience. But nescience is non-real and therefore does not import any real defect in the Self."[34] The same argument could be applied to all conditions, viz. (3) and (4) involving defect. In relation to (5) it is asked: "How can the Self, which is neither generality nor particularity, be the substrate?"[35] The answer: ". . . being determinable is not a condition for substrateness. What is needed for anything to be a substrate is the mere manifestation of immediacy; and

---

32. *Ibid.*
33. *Ibid.*, p. 14.
34. *Ibid.*, pp. 14-15.
35. *Ibid.*, p. 15.

this is established in the case of the self-luminous consciousness."[36]

The real issue, I think, is only faced towards the end when it is recognized that there may be a problem in drawing an analogy between the supersensible and the sensory — between the Self, etc. and shell-silver. Mahadevan raises the point thus:

> How is it possible, it may be asked, to superimpose egoism, etc. on the Self? In all cases of superimposition it is the same sense-organ that cognises both the substrate and the superimposed. For instance: it is the sense of sight through which both the "this" (nacre) and the silver are cognized. But this is not possible in the case of the Self since it is not a content of cognition of "this."[37]

He responds as follows: "In answer to this observation we say that it is not a requirement of superimposition that the substrate should be a content. What is required is only the presentation of the substrate and the superimposed as in union in a single cognition. And in the cognition "I" the Self and the not-Self in the form of the internal organ, are presented as in union. The Self, however, is not the content of this cognition. It is the internal organ, which is superimposed on the Self and bears the reflection of the Self, that appears in the form of the cognition "I.""[38]

What is significant about Mahadevan's treatment of the issue here is that he has used the shell-silver analogy in the context of the mutual superimposition of the *ātman* and the *ego* and not of the superimposition of the world on *Brahman*, as for instance in the case of Hiriyanna. The basic issue here needs to be clearly recognized. In the case of shell and silver

36. *Ibid.*
37. *Ibid.*
38. *Ibid.*

as an example of superimposition, the shell is a given object and silver superimposed on it. But consciousness, on which the superimposition, whether psychic of cosmic, is supposed to take place is never an object according to Advaita. How then can superimposition occur? "This objection is the very first that Śaṅkara raises against superimposition in the introduction to the Brahmasūtrabhāṣya, so one infers he feels it to be important. The bright pupil of the Upadeśasāhasrī I.1.2 also raises it."[39] According to Karl H. Potter,

> [Śaṅkara's] answer has several parts. First, though the Self is not an object of pure consciousness, it does not follow that it can't be the apparent object of empirical or ignorant awareness. Indeed, whenever we speak of ourselves in the first person as knower we are (though we do not know it) aware of the Self. Thus it is in a sense an object, although not of pure consciousness. Second, inasmuch as a person has ordinary awareness, which as we now know Advaita construes as a reflection of the "light" of pure Self, of pure consciousness, he is constantly aware of that "light," aware of pure consciousness, or *Brahman*, just as one who mistakes a rope for a snake is aware of the rope in a sense even though he calls it a snake. And third, there are types of error that do not seem to require that something be presented as an object on which to superimpose; consider our supposing that the sky is a blue-colored dome, whereas in reality there is only space (*ākāśa*). For Śaṅkara, apparently, *ākāśa* is not a presented object.[40]

---

39. Karl H. Potter, ed., *Advaita Vedānta up to Śaṅkara and his Pupils*, Delhi: Motilal Banarsidass, 1981, p. 94.

40. *Ibid.*, p. 94. The rest of the comment is also relevant here (*ibid.*, pp. 94-95): "This last response is not, I think, to be taken altogether seriously, inasmuch as Śaṅkara insists in other places that every awareness must have an *ālambana* or supporting object; since our →

While granting the vintage (from the Indian point of view) and vanguard (from the Western point of view) admonition that where if one cannot speak one must remain silent, has that point been reached[41] or is there a danger of premature closure here?

There are four metaphors which have been encountered in Śaṅkara's *adhyāsabhāṣya* up to this point: (1) of light and darkness; (2) of mother-of-pearl appearing like silver; (3) of moon, although one, appearing as double; and (4) of colourless space appearing as blue. Do these metaphors exhibit, perhaps by happy accident rather than subtle design, a gradual movement towards answering the basic question raised earlier? In the first case there is no logical basis for superimposition — the contrast is too stark. In the second case we have a plausible case of superimposition — the shell being mistaken for silver. In this example, however, superimposition involves conceptually both a subject and two distinct objects — shell and silver. In the next example, again a subject

---

→ blue-domed-sky awareness is an awareness that it must have a supporting object, namely *ākāśa*. Śaṅkara uses this realism to rebut the Vijñānavāda Buddhist in several places. The resolution of this apparent inconsistency on Śaṅkara's part can be found, I suspect, by reminding ourselves that though in one sense the object misinterpreted in superimposition must be really there to be misinterpreted, it doesn't follow that it must be "real" in the Advaitin's rather technical sense. Thus though in the cosmic projection there must be an analogous something for the world-illusion to be projected on, this something need not be pure consciousness or *Brahman* and indeed cannot be, insofar as we are speaking of and conceptualizing it. Granted we cannot explain that about which we cannot speak; the account seems to hang together with respect to that about which we can speak."

41. T.M.P. Mahadevan, *Superimposition in Advaita Vedānta*, pp. 16-17; M. Hiriyanna, *Popular Essays in Indian Philosophy*, p. 89.

and an object are involved — but the object has been reduced to one. In the last example this expository economy dispenses with the (sensory) object. In other words, we are only left with the subject in the end. The significance of this becomes clear when one realises that for superimposition to occur none of the five conditions discussed earlier in the case of the shell being mistaken for silver need be present. The conditions, briefly, were (1) the presence of residual impression, (2-4) defect in object of knowledge, cognized and instrument (*premeya-pramātr̥-pramāṇa doṣa*), and (5) cognition of generic feature of the substratum without the specific feature. The last example given by Śaṅkara was the blueness of the sky. Now consider the case of the perception of *ākāśa* as blue by all of us. To see *ākāśa* as blue is a case of error which takes place in spite of absence of conditions such as *pramāṇa-doṣa*, *prameya-doṣa*, and *pramātr̥-doṣa*. All of us see *ākāśa* as blue, though none of us suffer from any defect in the visual sense; and so there is not defect in the instrument of cognition. Since there is no similarity between *ākāśa* and blue colour, there is no defect in the object. Nor is there the defect in the cognizer such as fear, desire, etc. to be a condition of this error. Since this error takes place notwithstanding the absence of these conditions, it is wrong to say that these conditions are necessary for the occurrence of error.[42]

Or to paraphrase Śaṅkara's position: "Your alleged rule that one can superimpose an object only on another object that is before him has exceptions; we superimpose blue colour on *ākāśa* (the sky), which is not an object of perception. So our position is not inconsistent."[43] It is easier to recognize the full

---

42. R. Balasubramanium, *op. cit.*, pp. 95-96.

43. Karl H. Potter, ed., *op. cit.*, p. 120.

force of this argument when the distinction is drawn between the perception of colour in space possessing a *material* substratum and an *immaterial* substratum. Paul Deussen writes that "simple people transfer to space (*ākāśa*), which is not an object of perception, the dark colour of the ground and the like."[44] Here a material substratum is involved as compared with blueness perceived in the sky when an *immaterial* substratum will have to be postulated.[45]

We will now revert to the shell-silver metaphor. Even in this case, the given substratum alone, e.g. shell, will not do, even though it is necessary for the occurrence of error.

> *In addition to it, avidyā is required.* The substratum, whose generic feature alone is cognized without its specific nature and which does not undergo any change whatsoever, serves as the ground for the superimposition of an illusory object thereon by *avidyā* which undergoes modification. A material cause is one which has the capacity to give rise to an effect in its own being. If so, the substratum and *avidyā*, each in its own way, serves as the material cause. While the substratum which does not undergo any change is the transfigurative material cause (*vivartopādāna-kāraṇa*), *avidyā* which is subject to modification is the transformative material cause (*pariṇāmopādāna-kāraṇa*) of error. It is in the very being of the shell which is the unchanging substratum that the illusory silver appears. So shell is the transfigurative material cause of error since *avidyā* through modification projects the appearance of silver, it is the transformative material cause.[46]

These observations help in explaining the transition now to the discussion of *avidyā*.

---

44. Paul Deussen, *op. cit.*, p. 55 note 30.
45. Karl H. Potter, ed. *op. cit.*, p. 94.
46. *Ibid.*, p. 96, emphasis added.

The last section of Śaṅkara's Introduction to the *Brahma-Sūtra-bhāṣya* I would like to put under the metaphorical microscope is the one which follows the preceding one and introduces the concept of *avidyā*. Śaṅkara writes:

> This superimposition thus defined, learned men consider to be nescience (*avidyā*), and the ascertainment of the true nature of that which is (the Self) by means of the discrimination of that (which is superimposed on the Self), they call knowledge (*vidyā*). There being such knowledge, neither the Self nor the non-Self are affected in the least by any blemish or (good) quality produced by their mutual superimposition. The mutual superimposition of the Self and the non-Self, which is termed nescience, is the presupposition on which they base all the practical distinctions — those made in ordinary life as well as those laid down by the Veda — between means of knowledge, objects of knowledge (and knowing persons), and all scriptural texts, whether they are concerned with injunctions and prohibitions (of meritorious and non-meritorious actions), or with final release. But how can the means of right knowledge such as perception, inference, etc. and scriptural texts have for their object that which is dependent on nescience? Because, we reply, the means of right knowledge cannot operate unless there be a knowing personality, and because the existence of the latter depends on the erroneous notion that the body, the sense, and so on are identical with, or belong to, the Self of the knowing person. For without the employment of the senses, perception and the other means right knowledge cannot operate. And without a basis, (i.e. the body) the senses cannot act. Nor does anybody act by means of a body on which the nature of the Self is not superimposed. Nor can, in the absence of all that, the Self which, in its own nature is

> free from all contact, become a knowing agent. And if there is no knowing agent, the means of right knowledge cannot operate (as said above). Hence perception and the other means of right knowledge, and the Vedic texts have for their object that which is dependent on nescience. . . .[47]

If one were to continue to illustrate the *bhāṣya* with the help of the shell-silver metaphor one would have to say that "wherever there is *adhyāsa*, there is a confusion between two orders of being, we deduce that it presupposes ignorance. It is because we are oblivious of the shell that we see silver in its place. There are other causes also, such as the previous experience of silver, defective eye-sight, etc. to account for the mistake; but it will suffice for our purpose to confine our attention to the most important of them, viz. ignorance or *avidyā*."[48] This is precisely the direction in which Śaṅkara is moving. It was already noted earlier that in the end — with the last metaphor of the blueness of the sky — we were left with the subject and what we would normally call "illusion" but which Advaita insists is "superimposition." It involves *avidyā*. "Now *avidyā*, which is only another word for *ajñāna*, implies, like *jñāna*, some person to whom it belongs (*āśraya*) and some object to which it refers (*viṣaya*). The notion of "knowledge" is not complete until we mention the subject that knows and the object that is known. Similarly, in the case of *avidyā*, there must be someone whom it characterizes and an object which is misapprehended in it. In the present case, the person that mistakes the shell for silver is its *āśraya*, and the shell is the *viṣaya*."[49]

---

47. Elliot Deutsch and J.A.B. van Buitenen, *op. cit.*, pp. 152-53.
48. M. Hiriyanna, *Outlines of Indian Philosophy*, p. 353.
49. *Ibid.*

We have seen how *avidyā* may be considered the cause of silver earlier. It may now be noted that "it operates in a double manner. It conceals the fact of shell and shows up silver in its place. To see silver where there is only shell, a necessary condition is the concealment of shell. Suppression precedes substitution. These two aspects of it are respectively termed *āvaraṇa* or "veiling" and *vikṣepa* or "revealing." As the *avidyā* does not put the shell entirely out of sight, it is not lack of apprehension — a mere gap in thought — but misapprehension is therefore described as positive (*bhāva-rūpa*)."[50]

It is important here to introduce the distinction between contrary and contradictory. Extreme heat and extreme cold are contrary but they can be contradictory in the sense that one involves the denial of the existence of the other as such as when the same object is described as both at the same time. Now *avidyā* is "the contrary of *vidya*, not its contradictory; and the condition for the resulting error to disappear is the removal of *avidyā* which happens when *vidyā* arises in the self-same person in regard to the self-same object."[51]

What makes Śaṅkara's comment of particular interest is the fact that he locates the entire discourse about empirical knowledge in the domain of *avidyā*. The first point to note is that he does locate it in the empirical realm, the realm in which *avidyā* operates. For S. Radhakrishnan this is the significance of the metaphor of the shell-silver here and it carries two additional implications: (1) that the condition, like that of mistaking the silver in shell, is terminable; and (2) that the absolute is more real than the empirical realm.

---

50. M. Hiriyanna, *The Essentials of Indian Philosophy*, London: George Allen & Unwin, 1949, pp. 353-54.

51. *Ibid*.

> Even when the texts declare that the real is one and secondless, they do not contradict the empirical reality of the world we perceive. They only say that the reality of the world is not of an ultimate or absolute character. It is however beginningless and so is its cause, non-discrimination between the Self and the not-Self.
>
> Even when Śaṅkara says that *Brahman* appears as the world even as nacre appears as silver or as a single moon appears as having a second, he means that the manifestation is terminable. The world is subject to changes.
>
> Even as the nacre is more real then the silver, so the Absolute is more real than its manifestation. The manifestation is not devoid of reality for it is the combination of the real and the non-real, *satyānṛta-mithunam*.[52]

For some reason, Paul Deussen seems to want to exclude the Vedānta, as distinguished from *Mīmāṁsā*, from the realm of *avidyā*. "On the soil of this natural Ignorance stands according to Śaṅkara, all human knowledge, with the exception of the metaphysics of the Vedānta; thus, not only the empirical thought, that is, thought by means of the sense-organs, of common life, but also the whole ritual canon of the Veda, with its things commanded and forbidden under promise of reward and punishment in another world."[53] He goes on to say that:

> The immediate ground on which both worldly and Vedic actions must be referred to the sphere of Ignorance, lies in this, that both are not free from the delusion (*abhimāna*) of

---

52. S. Radhakrishnan, *The Brahma-Sūtra: The Philosophy of Spiritual Life*, London: Allen & Unwin, 1960, p. 233.
53. Paul Deussen, *The System of the Vedanta*, tr. By Charles Johnson, Chicago: Open Court, 1943, p. 56.

> seeing the "I" in the body; for neither knowledge nor action is possible unless one considers as belonging to the Self, the sense-organs and the body bearing them, and the ritual part of the Veda also cannot but transfer many circumstances of the outer world erroneously to the Soul.[54]

This amounts to saying that part of the shell is silver and the rest is mistaken for it. Not only are later Advaitins emphatic that Vedāntic discourse is included; in fact the text itself explicitly includes it by referring to all scriptural texts, specifically mentioning also those pertaining to *mokṣa*.

---

54. Vācaspati says that the knowledge that arises from a study of Vedānta is only as real as the nescience which it destroys. It is a product of nescience, because it is based on or presupposes the distinction between true knowledge, knower, and means of knowledge. But as soon as nescience is destroyed, the knowledge of *Brahman*, which is based on it, is also destroyed. According to Vācaspati, "the intuition of *Brahman*" uproots the entire "magical show of the world" including itself; . . . "K. Satchidananda Murty, *Revelation and Reason in Advaita Vedānta*, p. 101.

3

The Shell-Silver Metaphor in Advaita Vedānta

THE shell-silver metaphor is freely employed in Advaita Vedānta to illustrate the basic concepts of the system. These may be delineated as follows:

(1) As already discussed, it serves to illustrate the basic principle of *adhyāsa* or superimposition, as representing error as arising when different types of things are related in a judgment.

> In the example "this is silver," the "this" (i.e. shell) is empirically real and "silver" which is superimposed upon it is only apparently so. In other words, error is "illegitimate transference" or *adhyāsa* as Śaṅkara puts it in his celebrated Introduction to the *Vedānta-Sūtra*. Though the empirical and the apparent spheres are both objective, we, for the reasons assigned above, take that which is superimposed as less real than that on which it is. The falsity of such knowledge is not realized until we become conscious of the disparity between the objects related in it. When a person is seeing silver where there is only shell, he certainly does not know it to be false. On the other hand, he then feels convinced that it is quite as valid as any other knowledge. But when he approaches the object, picks it up and discovers that it is too light to

> be silver, he at once realizes that he was in error. What leads to the discovery is therefore this other knowledge whose object, because it is of the empirical kind, is not similarly sublated.[1]

(2) One may now inquire: what is the nature of the relationship between the shell and the silver?

> Now as regards the relation between the two terms involved in error: It cannot be identity, for things belonging to different levels of being cannot be identified. Nor can it be difference, for then the terms would not appear as subject and predicate in the same judgment as "This is silver." We cannot take it as identity-in-difference either, for that conception, as we shall see in the next section, is self-discrepant. The relation is therefore because it obtains between terms that belong to two different orders of being. The water that is quaffed in a dream will not quench actual thirst. At the same time the relation is not unreal for it is experienced. It is therefore like the lower of the two objects to which it relates, apparent, not empirical.[2]

It must be realized, however, that the negation may not always be that neat — that the same shell may *again* generate the illusion of silver. In such a case of recurrent or persistent illusion, inasmuch as the distinction between shell and silver was based on shell being realised on a lasting basis of which silver was a passing phase, to that extent "the distinction between objects of ordinary knowledge and those of illusion vanishes."[3]

1. M. Hiriyanna, *Outlines of Indian Philosophy*, pp. 351-52.
2. *Ibid.*, p. 352.
3. *Ibid.*, p. 350 note 2.

(3) If we regard silver as the lower of the two objects in relation to shell then we may further remark that the relation is such that

> "negating the higher of the two relata necessarily negates the lower. But the reverse is not true. If the shell is denied, the silver is not; but the negation of the silver is quite conceivable with the affirmation of the shell. This is what constitutes appearance. We accordingly describe the shell as the ground of which the silver is an appearance."[4]

(4) The metaphor also helps to explain the relationship between *Brahman* and the universe.

> "An illusory "silver" (*sukti-rūpya*) which is false, is always absent and therefore can be negated on its own support, the oyster shell (sukti). In the subsequent understanding, "It is not silver," the illusory "silver" is negated for all time (past, present, and future) on the very shell where it was known to exist. The world appearance is false to the Advaitins in the sense that with the final realization of *Brahman* it is negated on its own ground (*Brahman*)."[5]

One may begin by distinguishing between two forms of ignorance or *ajñāna* — total and partial. The idea of total ignorance may be related to "the reminiscent experience of a person who wakes up from deep sleep, viz. that he slept

---

4. M. Hiriyanna, *The Essentials of Indian Philosophy*, London: George Allen & Unwin, 1949, pp. 352-53.
5. Dinesh Chandra Bhattacharya, "Post-Śaṅkara Advaita," in Haridas Bhattacharyya, ed., *The Cultural Heritage of India*, Calcutta: The Ramakrishna Mission Institute of Culture, 1953, vol. III, pp. 265.

happily, and did not know anything.[6] The point to be pursued is the "exact meaning" of the description of ignorance as "not knowledge." "It may appear at first sight that it means the absence of all knowledge (*jñānābhāva*); but is cannot be understood in that sense for it would then be a mere blank, and such a state could not be recalled — much less as one of happiness. Hence the expression is taken to signify a unique type of *ajñāna* which, while it is totally removable by a right apprehension of ultimate reality, is distinct from the negation of knowledge."[7]

Clarity requires the simultaneous recognition of three points is this context: (1) that ignorance may be partial as in the waking state — we may (a) have knowledge of some things and not of others, e.g., we may know Jack lives but not where Jack lives; (b) we may mistake one thing for another, as a piece of shell for silver; (2) that our ignorance may be total as in deep sleep, when we do not know anything and at the time do not know that we do not know — unlike in the case of partial knowledge 1(a); (3) that inasmuch as the state of sleep is recalled, some form of latent knowledge in that comprehensive ignorance must have been present, similar to our realizing that the piece of shell mistaken for silver in case 1(b), was not silver.

In other words, there can be "units" of total ignorance (shell-silver) in partial ignorance, co-existing with units of correct knowledge (Jack lives) and absence of knowledge (where Jack lives), but there can be no units of partial knowledge or partial ignorance in total ignorance, although there may exist a latent total knowledge underlying it.

---

6. M. Hiriyanna, *Popular Essays in Indian Philosophy*, p. 86.
7. M. Hiriyanna, *The Essentials of Indian Philosophy*, London: George Allen & Unwin, 1949, pp. 88-89.

Furthermore, total ignorance can only be removed totally by knowledge and can only be removed successively, as when one wakes up from sleep or recognizes silver to be shell. In case of partial knowledge, however, knowledge and ignorance can simultaneously coexist — one can at the same time know Jack lives and not know where Jack lives.

One basic limitation of the shell-silver metaphor is that while it can clearly represent a "unit" of total ignorance within a frame of reference of partial ignorance and knowledge, it cannot represent total ignorance per se, except by miniscultization as when we might say that mistaking shell for silver is "deep sleep" and discovering it to be shell is an awakening. This explains why, when it is claimed that "there is no opposition between pure consciousness and nescience,"[8] one can argue that this is so because "nescience cannot have an independent existence outside consciousness"[9] and that "it is an internal fact always felt in association with consciousness"[10] when by nescience total nescience is meant. The case of deep sleep, for instance, "shows that pure eternal consciousness cannot be opposed to nescience. On the contrary it constitutes the only evidence of its being."

One may however ask: Granted that there is no opposition between pure consciousness and nescience. But how to account for the opposition of nescience as error with knowledge? It is felt beyond the shadow of a doubt that our erroneous perception of shell as silver is cancelled and corrected by knowledge of the shell in its true character. Our knowledge of shell is attended with the negative judgment "It is not

8. Nathmal Tatia, *Studies in Jaina Philosophy*, Banaras: Jain Cultural Research Society, 1951, p. 191.

9. *Ibid.*, p. 110.

10. *Ibid.*

silver." This shows that there is opposition between knowledge and error which is nothing but a species of nescience. This has puzzled many a respectable philosopher and it has been seriously asserted that the Vedantist is guilty of self-contradiction. But this is due to their failure to distinguish between knowledge and pure consciousness. Pure consciousness is an eternal and transcendental entity.

As regards nescience, it is also asserted by the Vedantist to be associated with the absolute consciousness which is pure and transcendental and undetermined by objective reference. There can be no difference in transcendental consciousness. The difference of one consciousness from another is only possible when it is made specific and particularized by objective reference, in other words, when it is possessed of a specific content and is called knowledge. Knowledge is consciousness in its essence, but it is different as a specific determination is from the genus. The opposition of error is with knowledge and not with pure transcendental consciousness which is rather the proof of it. Error is also a cognition with a distinct content and it is cancelled only by a cognition with an opposite content with reference to the same situation. It is the true cognition which cancels the false cognition. The true cognition is here called knowledge, and the false cognition error. The opposition only holds between them.[11]

It was pointed out earlier that the very fact that we are conscious of nescience shows that there is no opposition between them. But though a felt fact and uncaused entity existing concurrently with the Absolute, nescience is not regarded as an eternal verity like the absolute *Brahman*, because it is liable to be cancelled and corrected by the unerring realization of the nature of the self as identical with the

---

11. M. Hiriyanna, *The Essentials of Indian Philosophy*, London: George Allen & Unwin, 1949, pp. 191-92.

Absolute. It has been shown that nescience is destroyed by knowledge from the example of common error and its correction. The Vedantist deduces from the fact the conclusion that nescience is not a reality in the true sense of the term.[12]

In other words, the sublatability of partial error, when taken to indicate the sublatability of total error, serves to establish the non-eternal nature of ignorance and in this case it represents not the minisculization but the magnification of the shell-silver metaphor, which, though it cannot fully represent total ignorance because it is an instance of partial ignorance, generates the possibility of the removal of total ignorance.

If the argument is followed up and total ignorance is located in *Brahman* then the question of how the removal of one *jīva*'s *avidyā* does not liberate all will have to be answered differently. If *avidyā* is located in the *jīva*, then this is not an issue as other *jīva*s retain their *avidyā* while the liberated *jīva* loses his. But if it is located in *Brahman* then a different explanation is required. As located in *Brahman avidyā* is one and "it continues to exist even after a single individual's ignorance is destroyed through realization, just as a universal (*jāti*, e.g., cowherd) pervades all the existent individuals and is not affected by any change in their number."[13] The shell-silver metaphor will here apply in both the cases — depending on whether we locate the "silverness" in the eye of the beholder or in the shell itself.

The fact that there is no total *ajñāna* in sleep is also significant, for it forces Mīmāṁsā to describe error as partial knowledge.

---

12. M. Hiriyanna, *The Essentials of Indian Philosophy*, London: George Allen & Unwin, 1949, p. 190.
13. Dinesh Chandra Bhattacharya, *op. cit.*, p. 261.

Prabhākara does not admit that knowledge can ever play false to its logical nature.

> If so, it may be asked how we get the notion of Error at all in the common acceptance of that term. The answer is that in what passes for Error, we overlook the fact that there are two jñānas; and as a natural consequence of it, we also fail to notice the separateness of their respective objects. This failure to know, however, cannot by itself account for Error, for if it did, Error would be found to occur in sleep, which also is characterized by a similar absence of knowledge. This negative factor of failure should accordingly, in giving rise to Error, be viewed as operating with the positive one to which we have already referred, viz. the perception of the "this" as characterized by the features that are common to shell and silver. We may therefore describe Error as partial or incomplete knowledge; only in so doing, we must be careful to remember that, there is no single unit of knowledge here to which that term is applicable.[14]

One may remind oneself here of the objection raised in Advaita Vedānta: "how can there be reciprocal superimposition of the Self and the not-Self which are opposed to each other like light and darkness."[15] The answer to the objection ran as follows: they are not opposites. Rope and snake, or nacre and silver are not opposites; the former in each case serves as the substrate on which the latter appears. What are opposed to each other are the final mode of the mind which has taken on the form of the Self (*akhaṇḍākāra-vṛtti*) and the other modes of the mind which take the phenomena to be real (*viṣaya-vṛtti*s).[16]

Similarly one should note that "there is no antagonism between *avidyā* and self-shining *Brahman*, which is the locus

14. M. Hiriyanna, *Indian Philosophical Studies*, pp. 32-33.
15. T.M.P Mahadevan *Outlines of Hinduism*, p. 145.
16. T.M.P. Mahadevan, *Superimposition in Advaita Vedānta*, p. 4.

and revealer of *avidyā* (*ajñānāvabhāsaka*). It is the knowledge of *Brahman* which is antagonistic to and destructive of *avidyā*."[17]

The shell-silver metaphor explains the operation of *ajñāna* quite neatly at the empirical level as noted earlier, however, when it comes to *māyā*, the situation can get somewhat complicated. Hiriyanna clearly seems to accept Vācaspati Misra's view regarding the "duality of *avidyā*"; for —

> Vācaspati refers to two kinds of the indeterminable *avidyā*. One is the psychological *avidyā* in the form of *bhramaj-saṁskāras* (error impressions); and the other is the primal, positive *avidyā* which produces these beginningless series of delusions and *saṁskāras*. The latter is called *mūlāvidya* or the *kāraṇāvidyā* (primal nescience) which produces the former which is *tūlāvidyā* or *kāryāvidyā* (derivative nescience). These derivative individual ignorances are removable by the cognition of the true or real objects, while the primal nescience is destructible only by the cognition of the true or real object, viz. *Brahman*. This duality of *avidyā* and the plurality of the primal nescience are the distinctive features of Vācaspati's philosophy.[18]

For Hiriyanna goes on to say:

> It is the reference to a particular individual and to a specific object which this *avidyā* involves, that explains the uniqueness of the silver of which it is described as the source. Because it has a specific external object as its basis, the silver to which it gives rise appears out there — spatially determined — and is not a mere idea; and, because it has a particular person for its *āśraya*, the illusion which it occasions is special to him. It is this personal character that distinguishes private objects form the empirical ones which,

17. Dinesh Chandra Bhattacharya, *op. cit.*, p. 265.
18. Dinesh Chandra Bhattacharya, *op. cit.*, p. 267.

> as we shall see later, spring into being directly from *māyā* and are "public" or verifiable by others also. Though the objects we are now considering form an order by themselves, they are not altogether sundered from the other, for *avidyā* which occasions private objects is dependent upon the same source to which the common order of nature is due, viz. *māyā*, and is therefore described sometimes as *tūlāvidyā* or auxiliary *avidyā*. It is owing to this sameness of the source that when *māyā* is overcome in *mokṣa* both realms of objective being disappear alike. Otherwise though the common order of nature may cease to be then, the other might persist.[19]

However, the conclusion here is required by the premises, which if altered alters the conclusion.[20] If *avidyā* is located in *Brahman* then "*avidyā*" is one, the *jīva*s are many owing to the plurality of *antaḥkaraṇas*."[21]

19. M. Hiriyanna, *Outlines of Indian Philosophy*, p. 354.
20. See T.M.P. Mahadevan, *Superimposition in Advaita Vedanta*, pp. 29-30.
21. Dinesh Chandra Bhattacharya, *op. cit.*, p. 265.

4

The Complementarity of the Shell-Silver and the Rope-Snake Metaphors in Advaita Vedānta

THE rope-snake analogy is almost as popular as the shell-silver analogy in the exposition of Advaita Vedānta. If we compare the two, then the repulsiveness of the snake provides a contrast with the attractiveness of the silver. Inasmuch as the world is not so much frightening as alluring, it seems to confer some sort of advantage on the shell-silver analogy. Yet this attraction can turn out to be quite illusory. "As a snake perceived in the twilight may prove to be a rope (merely a harmless rope, yet it was taken for a snake and inspired fear), or as a glimpse of desirable silver may dissolve into a comparatively worthless piece of mother-of-pearl, even so the world, which inspires both fear and desire, may be caused to vanish into a neutral substratum."[1] In the end then one is left not with just the world but with the world of desire — of unfulfilled desire. It may even symbolise more than desire; the metaphor could even symbolise greed. "Superimposition is erroneous cognition (*mithyā-jñāna*), illusory appearance (*avabhāṣa*): It is the cognition of "that" in what is not-that." The stock examples are the rope-snake and the nacre-silver.

1. Heinrich Zimmer, *Philosophies of India*, edited by Joseph Campbell, New York: Pantheon Books, 1951, p. 419.

Snake is not rope; and yet a piece of rope is mistaken for a snake. Nacre is not silver; and yet the one who sees a shining object which is nacre lying on the sea-shore and imagines it to be silver, picks it up out of greed. These are cases of delusion, superimposition."[2]

Although the rope-snake and shell-silver metaphors are helpful by themselves in illustrating the existential situation from an Advaitic point of view, they are even more so taken together. The rope-snake metaphor invokes the psychology of revulsion in relation to *saṁsāra*; by contrast, the shell-silver metaphor connects with the psychology of attraction. These two constitute the kind of polarity (*dvandva*) which is intimately associated with saṁsāric existence, for "our acts are rightly or wrongly impelled by attachment and aversion; these are the twin forces that are responsible for the soul's performance of deeds. *Attachment and aversion are conditioned by the superimposition of attractiveness and repulsiveness of the objects*,"[3] i.e., the silver and the snake.

This polarity of being may be placed in an even broader context, as having to do with the similarity and differences between human beings and animals and with the release of human being from *saṁsāra*. The juxtaposition of the rope-snake and the shell-silver metaphor has enabled us to travel much further down the Advaitic road than would have seemed possible at first sight, by being respectively illustrative of repulsion and attraction. As Śaṅkara remarks:

> For this reason also: [worldly and Vedic knowledge belongs to the province of Ignorance], "because [thereby] no difference is made between man and animals. For just as animals, when for instance, a sound strikes their ears, in

2. T.M.P. Mahadevan, *Superimposition in Advaita Vedānta*, p. 1.
3. *Ibid.*, p. 21.

> case the perception of the sound is disagreeable to them, move away from it, and in case it is agreeable, move towards it, — as, when they see a man with an upraised stick before them, thinking: "He will strike me," they try to escape, and when they see one with a handful of fresh grass, approach him [one sees that when the Indian speaks of an animal, he thinks of a cow, somewhat as we think of a dog]: so men also whose knowledge is more developed (*vyutpanna-cittāḥ*), when they perceive strong men of terrible aspect, with drawn swords in their hands, turn away from them, and turn towards the contrary. Thus with reference to the means and objects of knowledge, the process in men and animals is alike. Of course in the case of animals, perception and the like goes on without previous (!) judgment (*viveka*); but as can be seen by the resemblance, even in the case of [spiritually] developed (*vyutpattimatām*) men, perception and the like for the time [of false knowledge] is the same; and if according to the spiritual canon the performance of works is permitted only to one who has gained insight (*buddhi*), and not to one who has not recognised the connections of the soul with the other world, yet for this permission it is not imperative that one [should have recognised] the truth concerning the soul freed from the Saṁsāra, to be taught by the Vedānta, which leaves behind hunger and the other [desires], and turns away from the difference between *Brāhmaṇa*s, warriors and the rest. For this truth is not implied in the injunction [of the work of sacrifice], but is rather in contradiction to it. And while the canon of ordinances is valid [only] for this degree of knowledge of the soul, it does not rise above the province of Ignorance.[4]

The shell-silver analogy also seems to be one which, unlike the rope-snake one, is capable of a dual application. When the

4. Cited in Paul Deussen, *op. cit.*, p. 57 note 34.

silver is recognized as shell, although its "silverness" is negated, its whiteness is not.[5] One could plausibly argue that what is given here — the shell — is not negated — only that element of which was taken as given of it but found not to be given namely, silverness. Just as, when the *jīva* is recognized to be *ātman*, the *jīva* is not negated but only those features of it which were really not given.

5. *Ibid.*, p. 16.

5

The Shell-Silver Metaphor in Sāṅkhya, Mīmāṁsā and Bhāskara

THE shell-silver analogy also helps clarify the theory of error as it is developed in Sāṅkhya. There are two versions of the theory to be found in Sāṅkhya — one in classical Sāṅkhya and the other as it is explained by Vijñānabhikṣu. And the difference between them can be clarified by the use of the shell-silver analogy.

The theory of error in classical Sāṅkhya can be explained with the help of two examples: that of the flower and the crystal and that of shell-silver. The first example refers to the fact that if a red flower is placed next to a white crystal, the crystal appears red. This is an error because the crystal is really white. Two points are worth noting here: (1) that both the flower and the crystal have to be actually present in this case for the error to occur, that is, the presence of both the objects is required as a condition for error, and (2) that the cause of error is the inability to distinguish between the two — between the flower as red and the crystal as white. The second example is provided by the shell-silver. In this case a piece of shell is mistaken for silver on account of its whiteness. Again two points are worth noting here: (1) unlike the case of the flower and the crystal in which *both* objects were present, in this although two objects are involved, that is, a piece of shell is mistaken for silver, only one object is actually present, the shell; (2) but as in the case of the crystal and the flower, the cause of error is the inability to distinguish between the two objects — the red flower and the white crystal in the first case and the shell and the silver in the second.

Vijñānabhikṣu, in his discussion of error, however, argues differently. In order to appreciate his argument it is necessary to recognize that in Sāṅkhya, perception is not direct, as in Nyāya-Vaiśeṣika, but takes place through the intervening agency of a psychic medium called *buddhi-vṛtti*. Of course the mind or *manas* is also considered as involved in perception in Nyāya-Vaiśeṣika but it is "merely the pathway of knowledge"[1] and hence passive. *Buddhi* in Sāṅkhya, however, is not conceived as "passive but endowed with a certain degree of self-activity, and as the abode of numberless impressions acquired through experience during a beginningless past."[2] In the act of knowing "the object and the particular bent of the *buddhi*, co-operate in all knowledge and the resulting image may not be, and generally is not, a complete copy of the former."[3] It is this *buddhi* with which the pure spirit, *puruṣa*, mistakenly identifies itself and taking on its features as its own suffers in the world, just as the pure crystal might imagine that it is bleeding because of its proximity of the red flower.

It is at this point that Vijñānabhikṣu introduces his own twist into the Sāṅkhya doctrine of error.

> The case of the "red crystal" is on a par with confounding the *buddhi* with Puruṣa and requires no special mention. The explanation of the "shell-silver" is interesting for, according to

---

1. M. Hiriyanna, *Indian Philosophical Studies*, p. 25.
2. *Ibid.*, pp. 25-26.
3. *Ibid.*, p. 26.

> Vijñāna-bhikṣu, it is not the "shell" alone that is given but the "silver" also is, in a sense: viz. as a mode of the *buddhi* through the revival of an old impression caused by the perception of the lustre. The confusion is thus between the shell which is actually given and "silver" which is given in the form of a *buddhi-vṛtti* or, as we might put it, between what is presented and what is represented. In other words, all erroneous knowledge is partially invalid and presents not merely what is but also what is not, which appears to be a somewhat startling conclusion for the Sāṅkhya to reach. We may add in conclusion that this later Sāṅkhya view of error is remarkably like that of Kumārila (*viparīta-khyāti*) while the previous one resembles that of Prabhākara (*akhyāti*).[4]

Two theories of error in Mīmāṁsā were mentioned above. They are also easily illustrated with the help of the shell-silver metaphor. The two well-known schools of Mīmāṁsā are the Prābhākara and the Bhāṭṭa. The Prābhākara school advocates the *akhyāti* view of error while the Bhāṭṭa school advocates what has been called the *vipritakhyāti* view of error. Wherein do these views differ?

The difference can again be explained with the help of the shell-silver analogy. M. Hiriyanna explains:

> In "shell-silver," for instance, there is something directly given, viz., the "this" but the "silver" is not so given. Yet it should not, on that account, be taken as "mental" or "non-existent"; for, its notion, being due to the suggestion of a former experience, goes back eventually to an objective counterpart. This view, like the previous one, splits up the object of erroneous knowledge into two parts — the "this" (*viśeṣya*) and the "what" (*prakāra*) and explains them separately. The first of them, as before, is not sublated when the mistake is rectified; and the explanation of the second element also is

---

4. M. Hiriyanna, *The Essentials of Indian Philosophy*, London: George Allen & Unwin, 1949, pp. 29-30.

> practically the same as before. Though not given here and now, the silver should have been experienced before; for otherwise it could not all have been fancied in the shell. The difference between the two views is that while according to *akhyāti*, Error is due to a losing sight of the fact that the presentative and the re-presentative factors stand apart unrelated (*asaṁsargagraha*); here in *viparita-khyāti*, it is ascribed to a wrong synthesis of them (*saṁsargagraha*). In the former case, Error, so far as that term is applicable at all, is an error of omission; because it only fails to grasp a part of what is given. So its discovery, when it takes place, does not mean the discarding as false of any feature previously cognized. Right knowledge may convey additional information about the reality in question; but it does not cancel any part of what is already known of it. In the latter, the Error becomes one of commission, for it includes as its content more than warranted in the reality that is presented, thus necessitating the subsequent rejection of a portion of it as false. In other words, illusion is here taken as unitary knowledge instead of as two *jñānas*.[5]

The two *jñāna*s here refer to (1) perception, and (2) memory. The Prābhākara school accepts the first: — "We feel 'this is the shell.' The same no doubt, cannot be said of the second *jñāna*, viz. memory, because silver is not found in the context. But in this it only exhibits its normal character; for, according to Prābhākara, all memory as such is invalid. That is, the former knowledge claims to be true and the claim is justified; the latter does not put forward any such claim at all. All knowledge, in this view, is of the one or of the other type; and there is none which may partake of the character of both."[6]

---

5. M. Hiriyanna, *Indian Philosophical Studies*, p. 34.
6. *Ibid.*, p. 32.

The *akhyāti* view is perhaps better illustrated by the analogy of the crystal and the red flower. "There also we have two *jñānas*, viz. the perception of the crystal *minus* its true colour and the sensation of *redness* alone in the flower. Each of these two *jñānas* is quite valid as far as it goes; only here both the *jñānas* are derived through the senses. As before they convey only a partial knowledge of the objects, viz. the crystal and the flower; but the basis of the Error here lies in the contiguity of the objects, not in their similarity."[7]

It is possible, however, to bring both the examples within the range of a single condition; that is to say, "both these conditions may be included in a single one: error is caused by mere (*kevala*) partial knowledge, which in the case of "shell-silver" means "nothing more than a knowledge of common features," and in the case of "red-crystal," nothing more than a knowledge of the positive features in question.""[8]

One curious consequence of the use of the shell-silver metaphor by both representatives of opposing schools of thought discloses parallels between their positions which might otherwise go unnoticed or undetected. For instance, Śaṅkara and Bhāskara, both of whom may approximately be placed in the ninth century CE[9] represent two very different approaches to Vedānta. Bhāskara is connected with *Brahma-pariṇāma-vāda*[10] which Śaṅkara criticizes;[11] and Bhāskara himself criticizes Śaṅkara whenever he can.[12] However, their positions come remarkably close in one respect in the

7. M. Hiriyanna, *The Essentials of Indian Philosophy*, London: George Allen & Unwin, 1949, p. 33.
8. *Ibid.*, p. 33 note 4.
9. M. Hiriyanna, *Indian Philosophical Studies*, p. 39.
10. *Ibid.*
11. M. Hiriyanna, *The Essentials of Indian Philosophy* , pp. 153-54.
12. M. Hiriyanna, *Indian Philosophical Studies*, p. 30.

discussion of the theory of error. The point at issue is: how does the silver come to be seen in the shell when it is really not there? "Bhāskara holds that the silver springs up, for the time being, where the piece of shell is. It may be difficult to conceive how it can do so, but that such was his view is not only implied by what he says in the *Bhāṣya*; it is also explicitly stated in some works of the other schools which refer to this point. Thus the Dvaita commentator Jaya-Tīrtha says: *Tatraiva tatkālikamut-pannaṁ* (*rajataṁ*) *saditi Bhāskaraḥ.*"[13] Students of Advaita will immediately recognize that the Advaitic explanation as offered by Śaṅkara follows the same lines for he claims "some kind of reality even for objects of illusion. . . we see the . . . silver."[14] The difference arises when it comes to the nature of reality which is claimed for it: it is *sat* or real for Bhāskara but *sadadavilakṣana* — other than *sat* and *asat* for Śaṅkara. But here again the difference can be overemphasized. Śaṅkara allows for three orders of reality and Bhāskara allows for only two. So in Bhāskara's scheme the impermanence of the silver is accepted but not its falsity. For him "contradiction does not signify the falsity of a thing."[15] Bhāskara contends that the idea of contradiction "is intelligible only in the case of the real which can be known, and not in that of the unreal which cannot be known"[16] and "since he recognizes no being intermediate between *sat* and *asat*, as Śaṅkara's *Advaita* does, he views whatever is experienced as necessarily real."[17] Śaṅkara would accord to it objectivity but not reality; or maybe only temporary

---

13. M. Hiriyanna, *The Essentials of Indian Philosophy*, London: George Allen & Unwin, 1949, p. 43.
14. M. Hiriyanna, *Outlines of Indian Philosophy*, p. 351.
15. M. Hiriyanna, *Indian Philosophical Studies*, p. 43.
16. *Ibid.*
17. *Ibid.*

"reality"[18] — but silver would slip out of the category of reality because for Śaṅkara impermanence implies falsity. For Bhāskara error "invariably points to a real object, though that object may be false when viewed from a particular standpoint. . . ." Thus in the case of the silver it "is quite real; but it is there for the time being and would be false only if viewed as what was originally given."[19] One might at this point suggest that —

> Another point requiring elucidation is why, if the silver is real as it is claimed to be, it is perceived only by the victim of the error and not by others. The only explanation conceivable is that Bhāskara regarded it as what is called a "private" object and not a "public" one, some of the causes giving rise to it (say, weakness of sight) being special to the person in question. A thing's being "private," it may be added, does not take away from it the reality. Our pains and pleasures are personal to each one of us, but they are not the less real on that account.[20]

Here again the point is both interesting and complex. In Śaṅkara one can distinguish between the public, the personal and the private. The *vyāvahārika* order of reality is public and our experience of it is personal; but the *prātibhāsika* order of reality such as dreams is private to us. However, it is worth noting that internal states such as pain etc. are experienced by us without the aid of the sense organs and so are dreams but the former are accepted as true and the latter as false! What makes the point even more interesting is that for Śaṅkara the proof of Realization is only subjective!

---

18. M. Hiriyanna, *Popular Essays in Indian Philosophy*, p. 91 note 1: "There is no objectivity without some kind of reality. That is what Śaṅkara means by saying that the *prātibhāsika* is also real."
19. M. Hiriyanna, *Indian Philosophical Studies*, p. 43.
20. *Ibid.*, p. 44.

6

The Shell-Silver Metaphor
Some Limitations

WE have so far focused on the versatile applicability of the shell-silver metaphor. The time may now be ripe to notice some of its limitations.

(1) One basic limitation of the shell-silver metaphor is that it is inherently idealistic, as compared to, say, the metaphor of the red flower and the crystal which is realistic. The point involved here is this; both the crystal and the red flower are present as distinct real objects — the error relates to the relationship between them when the crystal is perceived as red though it is not; the error does not relate to their reality as objects. In the shell-silver metaphor, however, only one of the two — the shell is actually present and the silver is imagined in it. In the first example the relata are real, the relationship is not; in the second example only one of the relata is real, but both the second object (silver) and its relationship to the silver are not.

This produces some interesting results in the use of the metaphor in Hindu thought, depending on whether it is appropriated by a realistic or an idealistic school within it.

> Thus focr the Bhāṭṭa school of Mīmāṁsā, which is realistic in its orientation, its use as an illustration of

> error creates a slight difficulty, because while realistic position suits cases like "red crystal," where the subject as well as the predicate is actually presented; but it is not adequate to explain those like the "shell-silver," where the predicative element, though presupposing a corresponding reality, eventually appears in a place where, and at a time when, it is not. That is, there is an additional subjective element here, which, however, is not in respect of silver as such, but as regards its "here-ness and now-ness" or its particularity. The silver itself, in its general or universal aspect, is real; only it is not found in the present context. If *viparīta-khyāti* should represent a realistic doctrine in spite of its admitting a subjective element of this kind, we have to understand it as maintaining the validity of knowledge whether it refers to an existing object or only to a subsisting one. In the example we are considering, the shell exists bearing the stamp of the particular time and place; but the silver only subsists in its non-temporal and non-spatial character, and knowledge in either case is equally valid.[1]

Thus, in a sense, then, the perception of silver in some way is in fact realistically acknowledged.

From an idealistic point of view, of course, one of the relata — the silver — is unreal, and so therefore is its relationship to the shell, which like *Brahman*, alone remains in the end as real, without any other relata or relationship.

(2) The next limitation of the shell-silver metaphor, despite its numerous advantages, arises from the fact that

---

1. M. Hiriyanna, *Indian Philosophical Studies*, p. 36.

although as an analogy it appeals to a fact of ordinary experience, it appeals to a fact of perceptual error rather than a normal verity. There are analogies from ordinary experience which may refer to normal veridical facts of experience and may be equally effective, as when we say that we can know a thing immediately without it being presented to us through sense-data, e.g. the fact that we have eyes or that we exist. It can therefore only illustrate metaphysical problems which correspond to a type of perceptual error. This should, however, not be taken to mean that the perceptual illusion as an analogy is to be underrated and that from normal experience overrated. This point would become clear if the usefulness of the first and the limitations of the second are suitably illustrated.

Let us first indicate the usefulness of the first as follows:

> The whole of the objective world is an appearance for it is the not-Self, like shell-silver. Here the analogy is drawn not from the sphere of normal experience, but from that of perceptual illusion. The falsity of the silver that may be seen where there is only shell is verifiable at the level of everyday experience; and there is consequently no difficulty in accepting it. But no such verification is conceivable as regards the falsity of the things constituting the not-self, so being as we continue to think under ordinary human conditions. Yet, if we extend to it on the basis of analogy the principle observed in the sphere of illusion, we may come to see that all that is objective, whether it is an adjunct of the self like the physical body or is a part of

> the external world like a jar, is an appearance. Such an argument may not give us certitude; but it can show that there is nothing necessarily absurd in the advaitic conclusion.[2]

Now the limitations of the normal illustration can be examined by citing the other famous maxim: "The body is not the self for it is knowable, like (say) a jar." It is not always realized that the statement is capable of two implications and that while the simple one remains in the realm of normal experience, the subtler one takes one beyond the strictly acceptable limits of logic in Advaita Vedānta.

> The general principle on which this argument is based, as indicated by the reason assigned, viz. knowability, is that the knower and the known are distinct or, more strictly, not identical — a principle which goes back to a much wider one that all transitive action involves elements which are not the same. The reasoning here may appear to involve no analogy, and therefore to be of the first type; but it is not so, for the contrast drawn in it is not between the knower and the known or the subject and the object, as required by the principle in question; it is between the components of the former, viz. the transcendental or ground self and the body, of which it is not the knower but merely the witness. Here the transcendental self, unlike the subject, is not accessible to common experience; and we are therefore transferring a principle which holds good in the empirical sphere to one beyond it. Hence the

---

2. M. Hiriyanna, *Indian Philosophical Studies*, p. 48. This passage has been cited earlier.

> reasoning is of the second type — namely, *sāmānyato-dṛṣṭa*, which represents a "variety of reasoning" not acceptable to the Advatin as "a *pramāṇa* in the strict sense of the term.[3]"

(3) Even as representative of perceptual error, the shell-silver metaphor suffers from a certain limitation inasmuch as its appeal is more tactile than visual in the matter of sublation. The standard example provided here is that when shell is mistaken for silver, "one thing here is mistaken for another, and the mistake disappears when it is known, say, that it is too light to be silver."[4] In the realm of sense perception, however, the relationship between touch and its elemental counterpart air is not as direct as between vision and form. Although this does not directly impinge on the analogical aptness of the shell-silver metaphor, nevertheless this "logical weakness" is worth keeping in mind *vis-à-vis* visual analogies. The epistemological problem at issue here may be clarified as follows:

> Qualities like odour and colour are found to inhere in substances like earth and fire; and it is said that we may deduce from it that the quality of touch or temperature (*sparśa*) also implies as its ground a substance, viz. air (*vāyu*). Here the qualities of odour, colour, etc. and the substances which they respectively characterize, viz. earth, fire, etc. are all perceivable; but air is not so, although the quality of touch may be. That is, we are extending here a principle verified in

3. M. Hiriyanna, *The Essentials of Indian Philosophy*, London: George Allen & Unwin, 1949, p. 47.
4. M. Hiriyanna, *The Essentials of Indian Philosophy*, London: George Allen & Unwin, 1949, p. 43.

> experience to something beyond it; and such an extension, according to Advaita, is not legitimate for in it we virtually jump from one particular to another, without passing through a general truth based upon actual observation, as we do in ordinary inference. It is, as the name given to it indicates, an inference which is based not on perception but on what is "seen from likeness" (*sāmānyato-dṛṣṭa*). Adapting the words which Śaṅkara uses in a similar context, we may say: If air also were perceivable like earth or fire, we might discover that touch was a quality of it. But, as a matter of fact, it is only touch that is perceived; and we cannot therefore decide whether it is connected with air as its quality, or with something else.[5]

(4) There is yet another limitation of the shell-silver analogy in relation to superimposition. According to Śaṅkara "If it be asked, "what is it that is called superimposition?" — the answer is: It is an awareness, similar in nature to memory, that raises on a different (foreign) basis as a result of some past experience."[6] Now in explaining the similarity of superimposition to memory the shell-silver illustration does help to show how this definition is not too wide, or that it avoids *ativyāpti*.

> If the definition of superimposition were this much alone, "the appearance elsewhere of what was seen before," it would be defective, being too wide (*ativyāpti*). There are cases of appearance elsewhere of what was seen before which are not cases of illusion. A person sees a particular cow; in it there

5. M. Hiriyanna, *The Essentials of Indian Philosophy,* London: George Allen & Unwin, 1949, pp. 45-46.

6. Swami Gambhirananda, tr., *op. cit.*, p. 2.

> is the appearance of "cow-ness." He then sees another cow in which also there is the appearance of "cow-ness." This is a valid cognition, and not a delusion. A man is seen at a certain place now and recognised as the same man seen earlier at another place. This, again, is appearance elsewhere of one who was seen before, which is valid. In order to avoid the contingency of the definition being too wide, Śaṅkara adds the phrase "of a nature like to that of recollection." When you recollect something, that thing is present in your mind, and does not appear before you. The non-presence of the object is the essence of recollection. As regards the appearance of cow-ness in the second cow and the appearance of identical person, seen before elsewhere, the objects are present, and so, they are not cases of recollection. In instances such as nacre-silver, what is seen now is not the same silver that was seen before. The apparent silver has a nature like that of recollection. *Hence, the definition is not too wide.*[7]

However, the analogy of shell-silver does not help in establishing the opposite — that the definition is not too narrow. It has been persuasively maintained that the definition is indeed not too narrow. Mahadevan demonstrates how it cannot be said that the definition is too narrow on the ground that it does not apply to some cases of delusion like dream-cognition.

> The recollected objects in dream, such as elephant, tiger, etc. are not present in dream. They are not reflected upon as having been seen earlier. On account of the defect present in the state of dream, there are superimposed on the objects the time and place where

7. T.M.P. Mahadevan, *Superimposition in Advaita Vedānta*, p. 2, emphasis added.

> they were formerly present and seen. Other cases of delusion, like the appearance of a shell as yellow on account of bile, or sugar tasting bitter on account of fever, should also be explained in a similar way. In all such cases there is appearance elsewhere of what was seen earlier, and the appearance has a nature which is like that of recollection. So, the definition is not too narrow; there is no non-pervasion (*avyāpti*).[8]

It is significant that all his illustrations here are interiorized, while the shell-silver represents an exteriorized illustration. And if superimposition were to be confined to such a situation it would have to be defined as follows: "It is an awareness, similar in nature to memory, that arises on a different external basis as a result of some past experience."

(5) As an example of individual perceptual error, the shell-silver metaphor tends to lean in the direction of individualism, though not necessarily solipsism. This becomes manifest in Hiriyanna's use of it as illustrative of *avidyā* when he has to deliberately move to check this drift. Thus he points out that

> *avidyā* is the contrary of *vidyā*, not its contradictory; and the condition for the resulting error to disappear is the removal of *avidyā* which happens when *vidyā* arises in the self-same person in regard to the self-same object. It is the reference to a particular individual and to a specific object which this *avidyā* involves that explains the uniqueness of the silver of which it is described as the source. Because it has a specific external object as its basis, the silver to which

8. M. Hiriyanna, *The Essentials of Indian Philosophy*, London: George Allen & Unwin, 1949.

> it gives rise appears out there — spatially determined — and is not a mere idea; and, because it has a particular person for its *āśraya*, the illusion which it occasions is special to him. It is this personal character that distinguishes private objects from the empirical ones which, as we shall see later, spring into being directly from *māyā* and are "public" or verifiable by others also.[9]

Even if we regard "*avidyā*s associated with individual selves" as "parts or phases"[10] of *māyā*, it could be maintained that —

> Each part of *avidyā* gives rise to a separate and distinct world. The whole world of sense and activity is restricted to each person and produced by the *avidyā* residing in that particular person, even as the merely apparent silver (perceived in place of the shell) is different for each observer and is produced by the *avidyā* residing in each observer. . . . But that these many worlds should appear to be one, is a pure misapprehension similar to that expressed in the words, "I too saw the very same silver which you saw."[11]

---

9. M. Hiriyanna, *Outlines of Indian Philosophy*, p. 354. This passage has been cited earlier.
10. M. Hiriyanna, *The Essentials of Indian Philosophy*, p. 163.
11. S. Radhakrishnan, *Indian Philosophy*, London: George Allen & Unwin, 1962, vol. II, p. 612.

Conclusion

THE discourse of Advaita Vedānta employs several metaphors to render its doctrines comprehensible, or at least credible. Both the variety of such metaphors, as that of snake-rope, shell-silver, reflections, dreams and so on[1] and the versatility of their application to explain different aspects of Advaitic doctrines imparts a certain tentativeness to the texture of its discourse which is somewhat at odds with its insistence on Vedic authority as the basis of its doctrines. The fact that it places the Vedas themselves in the realm of *mithyā* further adds to the intellectual intrigue of the issue.

This diversity or multiplicity of ways utilized to point to the unicity of the ultimate reality of *Brahman* becomes less baffling if we consider it as trying to point to this ultimate reality from within a world of multiplicity, so that its discourse within it partakes of the same quality. The way out of the water to the shore also involves wading through that very water.[2]

---

1. See John Grimes, *The Vivekacūḍāmaṇi of Śaṅkaracārya Bhagavatpāda: An Introduction and Translation*, Hants, England: Ashgate Publishing Limited, 2004, p. 163; etc.
2. Chakravarthi Ram Prasad, *Advaita Epistemology and Metaphysics: An Outline of Indian Non-Realism*, London: Routledge Curzon, 2002) pp. 3-4.

Bibliography

Balasubramaniam, R., 1976, *Advaita Vedānta*, Madras: University of Madras.

Deussen, Paul, 1943, *The System of the Vedānta*, tr. By Charles Johnson. Chicago: Open Court.

Deutsch, Eliot and Van Buitenen, J.A.B., eds., 1971, *A Source Book of Advaita Vedānta*, Honolulu: The University Press of Hawaii.

Fort, Andrew O., 1990, *The Self and Its States: A State of Consciousness Doctrine in Advaita Vedānta*, Delhi: Motilal Banarasidass.

———, 1998, *Jīvanmukti in Transformation: Embodied Liberation in Advaita and Neo-Vedānta*, Albany, New York: State University of New York Press.

Gambhirananda, Swami, tr., 1977, *Brahma-Sūtra-Bhāṣya of Śrī Śaṅkarācārya*, Calcutta: Advaita Ashrama.

Grimes, John, 2004, *The Vivekacūḍāmaṇi of Śaṅkarācārya Bhagavatpāda: An Introduction and Translation*. Hants, England: Ashgate Publishing Limited.

Hiriyanna, M., 1932, *Outlines of Indian Philosophy*, London: George Allen & Unwin.

———, 1949, *The Essentials of Indian Philosophy*, London: Allen & Unwin.

———, 1952, *Popular Essays in Indian Philosophy*, Mysore: Kavyalaya Publishers.

———, 1957, *Indian Philosophical Studies*, Mysore: Kavyalaya Publishers.

Mahadevan, T.M.P., 1971, *Outlines of Hinduism*, Bombay: Chetana Ltd.

———, 1985, *Superimposition in Advaita Vedānta*, New Delhi: Sterling Publishers Private Ltd.

Murty, K. Satchidananda, 1974, *Revelation and Reason in Advaita Vedānta*, Delhi: Motilal Banarasidass.

Potter, Karl H., ed., 1981, *Advaita Vedānta Up To Śaṅkara and His Pupils*, Delhi: Motilal Banarasidass.

Radhakrishnan, S., ed., 1996 [1953], *The Principal Upaniṣads*, Atlantic Heights, N.J.: Humanities Press.

———, 1960, *The Brahma-Sūtra: The Philosophy of Spiritual Life*, London: Allen & Unwin.

———, 1962, *Indian Philosophy*, vol. II, London: George Allen & Unwin.

Ram-Prasad, Chakravarthi, 2002, *Advaita Epistemology and Metaphysics: An Outline of Indian Non-Realism*. London: Routledge Curzon.

Rambachan, Anantanand, 1991, *Accomplishing the Accomplished: The Vedas, as a Source of Valid Knowledge in Śaṅkara*, Honolulu: University of Hawaii Press.

Singh, B.N., 1986, *Indian Logic*, Varanasi: Asha Prakashan.

Tatia, Nathmal, 1951, *Studies in Jaina Philosophy*, Banaras: Jain Cultural Research Society.

Zimmer, Heinrich, 1951, *Philosophies of India*, Edited by Joseph Campbell. New York: Pantheon Books.

Author Index

Subject Index